Piano
Advanced
Chords

Easy to Use, Easy to Carry
One Chord on Every Page

Jake Jackson

Flame Tree
Music

FLAME TREE
PUBLISHING

Publisher & Creative Director: Nick Wells
Editors: Polly Prior and Catherine Taylor
Designer and diagrams: Jake

This edition first published 2012 by
FLAME TREE PUBLISHING
6 Melbray Mews
Fulham, London SW6 3NS
United Kingdom
www.flametreepublishing.com

Music website: www.flametreemusic.com

Flame Tree Publishing is an imprint of Flame Tree Publishing Ltd

© 2012 this edition Flame Tree Publishing Ltd

18 20 22 21 19
3 5 7 9 10 8 6 4 2

ISBN 978-0-85775-375-5

A CIP record for this book is available from the
British Library upon request.

All rights reserved. No part of this publication may be reproduced,
stored in a retrieval system, or transmitted in any form or by any means,
electronic, mechanical, photocopying, recording or otherwise, without the
prior permission in writing of the publisher.

Acknowledgements
All images and notation © copyright **Foundry Arts** 2012

Jake Jackson is a musician and writer of practical music books.
His publications include *Advanced Guitar Chords*; *Beginner's
Guide to Reading Music*; *Chords for Kids*; *Classic Riffs*; *Guitar
Chords*; *How to Play Electric Guitar*; *Piano & Keyboard
Chords*; *Scales and Modes* and *The Songwriter's Rhyming
Dictionary*. Jake's album 'Jakesongs' is available on on iTunes,
Amazon, Spotify and LastFM.

Printed in China

Introduction

The keyboard diagrams in this book will help you to learn the shapes of all the chords, and will be a useful reference guide when you are playing and composing your own music. This will enable you to explore new ways of making music and is particularly useful in a band setting.

This new book is a companion to the original **Piano & Keyboard Chords** title which covered the basic chords, including majors, minors and sevenths. **Advanced Piano Chords** introduces ninths, elevenths and thirteenth chords with a range of other useful stylings that will add musical interest to any composition or improvisation. As before, the left-hand page offers finger positions for the left hand, the right-hand page presents right hand positions.

This series of practical music books is linked to **www.flametreemusic.com** which provides an extensive range of chords, with sounds for both piano and guitar, to offer the musician an excellent musical resource.

Page Layout

Advanced Piano Chords is divided into keys, which are easily accessible using the **tabs** along the edge of the page. The diagram for each chord is shown with a suggested key (root) note position for the **left hand** on the **left-hand page** and either the main triad or the balance of the notes to be played with the **right hand**, on the **right-hand page**.

Name and abbreviation of the chord.

Use the tabs on the side of each page to find the key you want quickly.

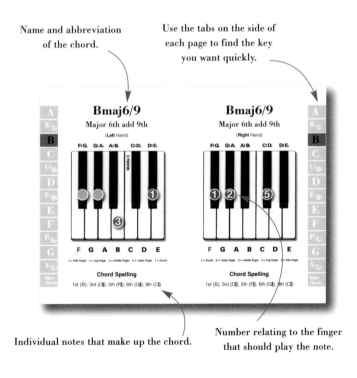

Individual notes that make up the chord.

Number relating to the finger that should play the note.

Which Finger Shall I Use?

Each diagram suggests which finger to use to play each note of the chord. **Each page** has a **fingering guide** below the diagram. The **blue circles** on the **left-hand page** suggest which finger could be used to play the notes in the left hand. **Pale blue circles** show notes that can be played **in addition** to the **root** note, or **instead of** the root note to create an inverted chord style. The notes to be played in the **right hand** will be shown in **red circles** on the right-hand page.

Left-hand notes
are blue.

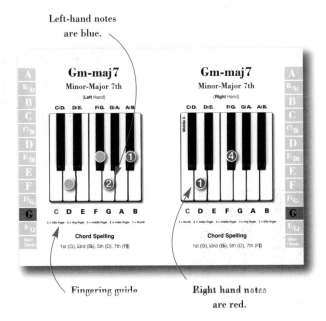

Fingering guide

Right hand notes
are red.

The Note Names

Although the names of the notes are included above and below each keyboard diagram, it is useful to show them here too as a reminder, with the **sharps** and **flats** (or black notes) on separate diagrams.

The White Notes
(naturals)

The Black Notes
(sharps/♯)

The Black Notes
(flats/♭)

Inversions

The last section of the book features the first inversions of some of the chords. Inversions are used to provide additional colour to a harmony. They are chords which do not have their key (root) note as the bass (or bottom) note. For example, in its root (or normal) position, the chord of C major is made up of the key note (**C**) with the third (**E**) and fifth (**G**) notes above it.

C Major

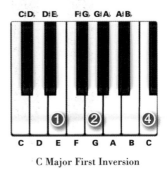

C Major First Inversion

The first inversion of C major consists of **E** at the **bottom** with the notes **G** and **C** above it. The second inversion would use the fifth as the root note, (in this case **G**).

First inversions of the **major 6th add 9th, minor 6th add 9th, major 9th** and **minor 9th** chords have been included. Using the method above, every chord in this book can be inverted.

A

B♭/A♯

B

C

C♯/D♭

D

E♭/D♯

E

F

F♯/G♭

G

A♭/G♯

Other Chords

Amaj6/9

Major 6th add 9th

(**Left** Hand)

C♯D♭   D♯E♭   F♯G♭ G♯A♭ A♯B♭

C   D   E   F   G   A   B

5 = little finger 4 = ring finger 3 = middle finger 2 = index finger 1 = thumb

Chord Spelling

1st (A), 3rd (C♯), 5th (E), 6th (F♯), 9th (B)

Amaj6/9
Major 6th add 9th
(**Right** Hand)

A

B♭/A♯

B

C

C♯/D♭

D

E♭/D♯

E

F

F♯/G♭

G

A♭/G♯

Other Chords

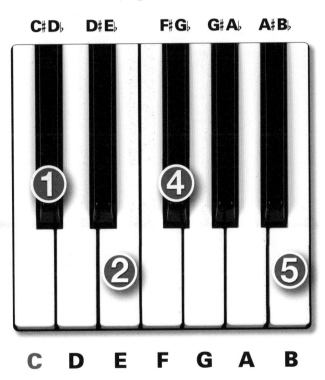

C♯D♭   D♯E♭   F♯G♭   G♯A♭   A♯B♭

C   D   E   F   G   A   B

1 = thumb   2 = index finger   3 = middle finger   4 = ring finger   5 = little finger

Chord Spelling

1st (A), 3rd (C♯), 5th (E), 6th (F♯), 9th (B)

B♭/A#
B
C
C#/D♭
D
E♭/D#
E
F
F#/G♭
G
A♭/G#
Other Chords

Am6/9

Minor 6th add 9th

(**Left** Hand)

C#D♭ D#E♭ F#G♭ G#A♭ A#B♭

C   D   E   F   G   A   B

5 = little finger   4 = ring finger   3 = middle finger   2 = index finger   1 = thumb

Chord Spelling

1st (A), ♭3rd (C), 5th (E), 6th (F#), 9th (B)

Am6/9

Minor 6th add 9th

(**Right** Hand)

1 = thumb   2 = index finger   3 = middle finger   4 = ring finger   5 = little finger

Chord Spelling

1st (A), ♭3rd (C), 5th (E), 6th (F♯), 9th (B)

A6sus4

6th Suspended 4th

(**Left** Hand)

C♯D♭ D♯E♭ F♯G♭ G♯A♭ A♯B♭

C D E F G A B

5 = little finger   4 = ring finger   3 = middle finger   2 = index finger   1 = thumb

Chord Spelling

1st (A), 4th (D), 5th (E), 6th (F♯)

A
B♭/A♯
B
C
C♯/D♭
D
E♭/D♯
E
F
F♯/G♭
G
A♭/G♯
Other Chords

A6sus4

6th Suspended 4th

(Right Hand)

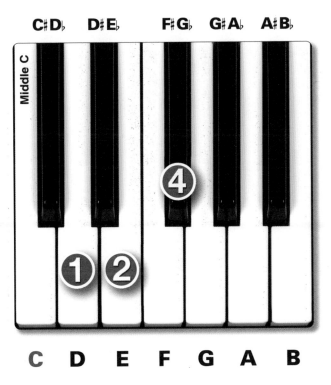

A

B♭/A♯

B

C

C♯/D♭

D

E♭/D♯

E

F

F♯/G♭

G

A♭/G♯

Other Chords

1 = thumb   2 = index finger   3 = middle finger   4 = ring finger   5 = little finger

Chord Spelling

1st (A), 4th (D), 5th (E), 6th (F♯)

A

B♭/A♯

B

C

C♯/D♭

D

E♭/D♯

E

F

F♯/G♭

G

A♭/G♯

Other
Chords

Amaj7+5

Major 7th Augmented 5th

(**Left** Hand)

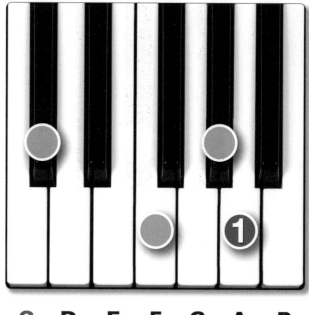

C♯D♭   D♯E♭   F♯G♭   G♯A♭   A♯B♭

C   D   E   F   G   A   B

5 = little finger   4 = ring finger   3 = middle finger   2 = index finger   1 = thumb

Chord Spelling

1st (A), 3rd (C♯), ♯5th (E♯), 7th (G♯)

Amaj7+5

Major 7th Augmented 5th

(**Right** Hand)

1 = thumb   2 = index finger   3 = middle finger   4 = ring finger   5 = little finger

Chord Spelling

1st (A), 3rd (C♯), ♯5th (E♯), 7th (G♯)

A

B♭/A♯

B

C

C♯/D♭

D

E♭/D♯

E

F

F♯/G♭

G

A♭/G♯

Other Chords

B♭/A#
B
C
C#/D♭
D
E♭/D#
E
F
F#/G♭
G
A♭/G#
Other Chords

Amaj7sus4

Major 7th Suspended 4th

(**Left** Hand)

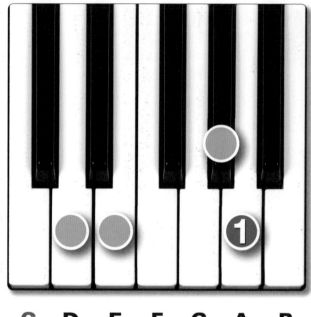

5 = little finger   4 = ring finger   3 = middle finger   2 = index finger   1 = thumb

Chord Spelling

1st (A), 4th (D), 5th (E), 7th (G#)

Amaj7sus4

Major 7th Suspended 4th

(**Right** Hand)

A

B♭/A♯

B

C

C♯/D♭

D

E♭/D♯

E

F

F♯/G♭

G

A♭/G♯

Other Chords

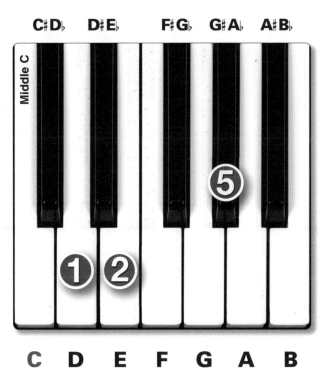

C♯D♭   D♯E♭   F♯G♭   G♯A♭   A♯B♭

Middle C

C   D   E   F   G   A   B

1 = thumb   2 = index finger   3 = middle finger   4 = ring finger   5 = little finger

Chord Spelling

1st (A), 4th (D), 5th (E), 7th (G♯)

A

Bb/A#

B

C

C#/Db

D

Eb/D#

E

F

F#/Gb

G

Ab/G#

Other Chords

Am-maj7
Minor-Major 7th

(**Left** Hand)

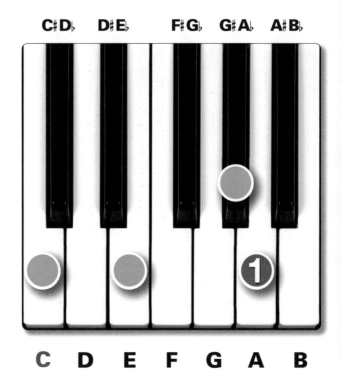

C#Db   D#Eb   F#Gb   G#Ab   A#Bb

C   D   E   F   G   A   B

5 = little finger   4 = ring finger   3 = middle finger   2 = index finger   1 = thumb

Chord Spelling

1st (A), b3rd (C), 5th (E), 7th (G#)

Am-maj7

Minor-Major 7th

(**Right** Hand)

A

B♭/A♯

B

C

C♯/D♭

D

E♭/D♯

E

F

F♯/G♭

G

A♭/G♯

Other Chords

C♯D♭   D♯E♭   F♯G♭   G♯A♭   A♯B♭

Middle C

C   D   E   F   G   A   B

1 = thumb   2 = index finger   3 = middle finger   4 = ring finger   5 = little finger

Chord Spelling

1st (A), ♭3rd (C), 5th (E), 7th (G♯)

Amaj9
Major 9th

(**Left** Hand)

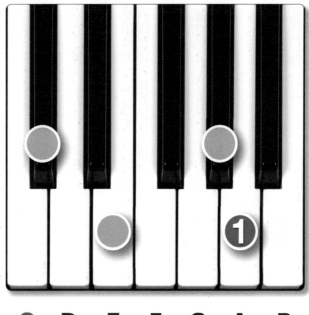

5 = little finger   4 = ring finger   3 = middle finger   2 = index finger   1 = thumb

Chord Spelling

1st (A), 3rd (C♯), 5th (E), 7th (G♯), 9th (B)

Amaj9
Major 9th

(**Right** Hand)

A

B♭/A♯

B

C

C♯/D♭

D

E♭/D♯

E

F

F♯/G♭

G

A♭/G♯

Other Chords

C♯D♭   D♯E♭   F♯G♭   G♯A♭   A♯B♭

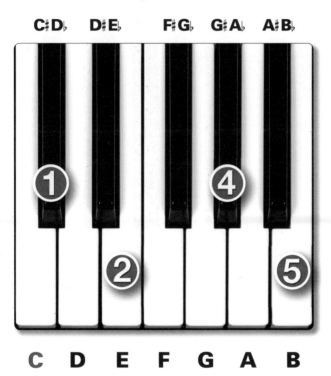

C   D   E   F   G   A   B

1 = thumb   2 = index finger   3 = middle finger   4 = ring finger   5 = little finger

Chord Spelling

1st (A), 3rd (C♯), 5th (E), 7th (G♯), 9th (B)

Am9

Minor 9th

(**Left** Hand)

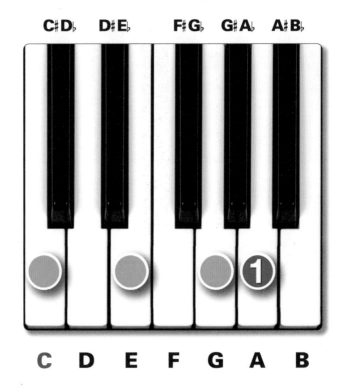

5 = little finger 4 = ring finger 3 = middle finger 2 = index finger 1 = thumb

Chord Spelling

1st (A), ♭3rd (C), 5th (E), ♭7th (G), 9th (B)

Am9

Minor 9th

(**Right** Hand)

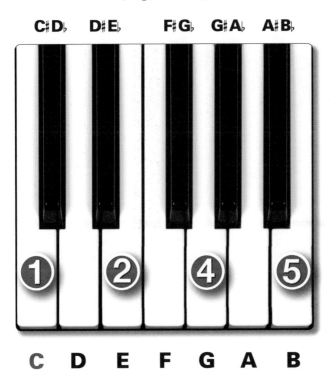

C♯D♭ D♯E♭ F♯G♭ G♯A♭ A♯B♭

C D E F G A B

1 = thumb 2 = index finger 3 = middle finger 4 = ring finger 5 = little finger

Chord Spelling

1st (A), ♭3rd (C), 5th (E), ♭7th (G), 9th (B)

A

B♭/A♯

B

C

C♯/D♭

D

E♭/D♯

E

F

F♯/G♭

G

A♭/G♯

Other Chords

Am-maj9
Minor-Major 9th

(**Left** Hand)

Bb/A#
B
C
C#/Db
D
Eb/D#
E
F
F#/Gb
G
Ab/G#
Other Chords

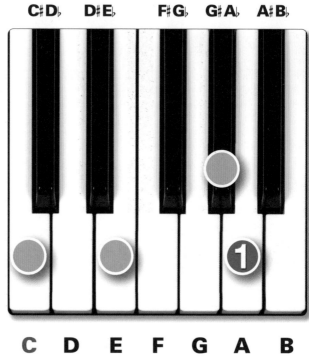

5 = little finger   4 = ring finger   3 = middle finger   2 = index finger   1 = thumb

Chord Spelling

1st (A), b3rd (C), 5th (E), 7th (G#), 9th (B)

Am-maj9
Minor-Major 9th
(**Right** Hand)

A

B♭/A♯

B

C

C♯/D♭

D

E♭/D♯

E

F

F♯/G♭

G

A♭/G♯

Other Chords

1 = thumb   2 = index finger   3 = middle finger   4 = ring finger   5 = little finger

Chord Spelling

1st (A), ♭3rd (C), 5th (E), 7th (G♯), 9th (B)

A

B♭/A♯

B

C

C♯/D♭

D

E♭/D♯

E

F

F♯/G♭

G

A♭/G♯

Other
Chords

Amaj11
Major 11th

(**Left** Hand)

F♯G♭ G♯A♭ A♯B♭ C♯D♭ D♯E♭

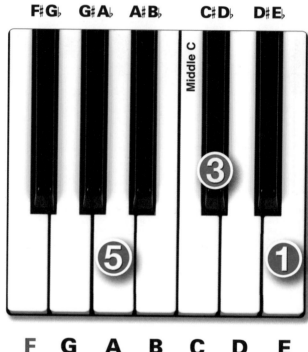

F G A B C D E

5 = little finger 4 = ring finger 3 = middle finger 2 = index finger 1 = thumb

Chord Spelling

1st (A), 3rd (C♯), 5th (E), 7th (G♯),
9th (B), 11th (D)

Amaj11

Major 11th

(**Right** Hand)

A
Bb/A#
B
C
C#/Db
D
Eb/D#
E
F
F#/Gb
G
Ab/G#
Other Chords

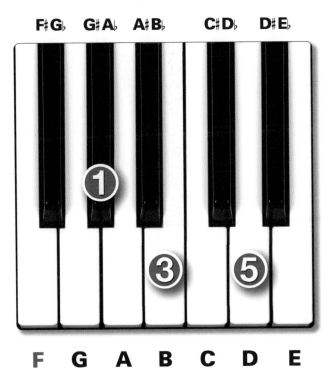

F#Gb G#Ab A#Bb   C#Db   D#Eb

F G A B C D E

1 = thumb   2 = index finger   3 = middle finger   4 = ring finger   5 = little finger

Chord Spelling

1st (A), 3rd (C#), 5th (E), 7th (G#),
9th (B), 11th (D)

Bb/A#
B
C
C#/Db
D
Eb/D#
E
F
F#/Gb
G
Ab/G#
Other Chords

Am11

Minor 11th

(**Left** Hand)

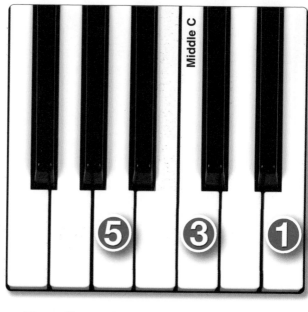

F#Gb G#Ab A#Bb   C#Db   D#Eb

Middle C

F   G   A   B   C   D   E

5 = little finger   4 = ring finger   3 = middle finger   2 = index finger   1 = thumb

Chord Spelling

1st (A), b3rd (C), 5th (E), b7th (G),
9th (B), 11th (D)

Am11

Minor 11th

(**Right** Hand)

A

Bb/A#

B

C

C#/Db

D

Eb/D#

E

F

F#/Gb

G

Ab/G#

Other
Chords

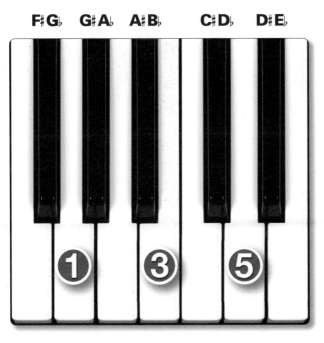

F#Gb   G#Ab   A#Bb   C#Db   D#Eb

① ③ ⑤

F   G   A   B   C   D   E

1 = thumb   2 = index finger   3 = middle finger   4 = ring finger   5 = little finger

Chord Spelling

1st (A), b3rd (C), 5th (E), b7th (G),
9th (B), 11th (D)

A11

Dominant 11th

(**Left** Hand)

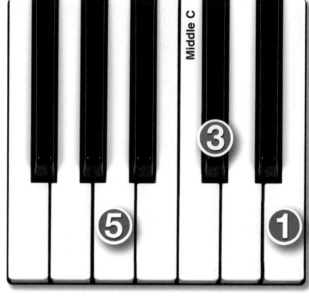

F#G♭   G#A♭   A#B♭   C#D♭   D#E♭

Middle C

F   G   A   B   C   D   E

5 = little finger   4 = ring finger   3 = middle finger   2 = index finger   1 = thumb

Chord Spelling

1st (A), 3rd (C#), 5th (E), ♭7th (G),
9th (B), 11th (D)

A

B♭/A#

B

C

C#/D♭

D

E♭/D#

E

F

F#/G♭

G

A♭/G#

Other
Chords

A11

Dominant 11th

(**Right** Hand)

F#G♭   G#A♭   A#B♭   C#D♭   D#E♭

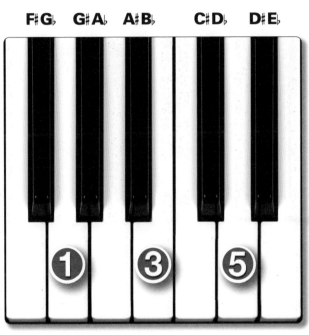

F   G   A   B   C   D   E

1 = thumb   2 = index finger   3 = middle finger   4 = ring finger   5 = little finger

A

B♭/A#

B

C

C#/D♭

D

E♭/D#

E

F

F#/G♭

G

A♭/G#

Other
Chords

Chord Spelling

1st (A), 3rd (C#), 5th (E), ♭7th (G),
9th (B), 11th (D)

B♭/A♯
B
C
C♯/D♭
D
E♭/D♯
E
F
F♯/G♭
G
A♭/G♯
Other Chords

Amaj13

Major 13th

(**Left** Hand)

G♯A♭   A♯B♭   C♯D♭   D♯E♭   F♯G♭

Middle C

③ ⑤ ①

A   B   C   D   E   F   G

5 = little finger   4 = ring finger   3 = middle finger   2 = index finger   1 = thumb

Chord Spelling

1st (A), 3rd (C♯), 5th (E), 7th (G♯),
9th (B), 11th (D), 13th (F♯)

Amaj13
Major 13th

(**Right** Hand)

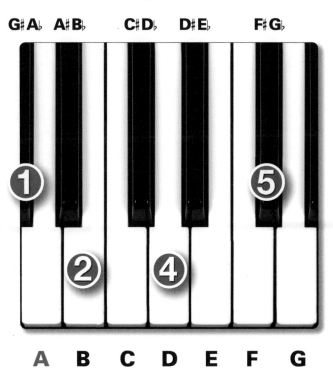

1 = thumb   2 = index finger   3 = middle finger   4 = ring finger   5 = little finger

Chord Spelling

1st (A), 3rd (C♯), 5th (E), 7th (G♯),
9th (B), 11th (D), 13th (F♯)

A
B♭/A♯
B
C
C♯/D♭
D
E♭/D♯
E
F
F♯/G♭
G
A♭/G♯
Other Chords

A

B♭/A♯

B

C

C♯/D♭

D

E♭/D♯

E

F

F♯/G♭

G

A♭/G♯

Other
Chords

Am13

Minor 13th

(**Left** Hand)

G♯A♭ A♯B♭   C♯D♭   D♯E♭   F♯G♭

Middle C

⑤   ④   ②   ①

A   B   C   D   E   F   G

5 = little finger   4 = ring finger   3 = middle finger   2 = index finger   1 = thumb

Chord Spelling

1st (A), ♭3rd (C), 5th (E), ♭7th (G),
9th (B), 11th (D), 13th (F♯)

Am13

Minor 13th

(**Right** Hand)

1 = thumb   2 = index finger   3 = middle finger   4 = ring finger   5 = little finger

Chord Spelling

1st (A), ♭3rd (C), 5th (E), ♭7th (G),
9th (B), 11th (D), 13th (F♯)

A
B♭/A♯
B
C
C♯/D♭
D
E♭/D♯
E
F
F♯/G♭
G
A♭/G♯
Other Chords

A

B♭/A♯

B

C

C♯/D♭

D

E♭/D♯

E

F

F♯/G♭

G

A♭/G♯

Other
Chords

A13

Dominant 13th

(**Left** Hand)

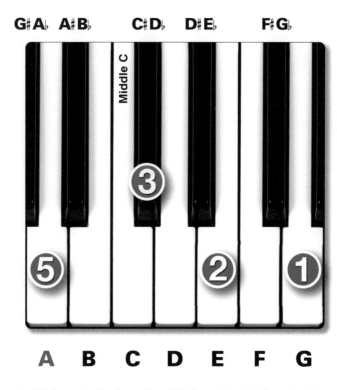

G♯A♭   A♯B♭   C♯D♭   D♯E♭   F♯G♭

Middle C

③

⑤   ②   ①

A   B   C   D   E   F   G

5 = little finger   4 = ring finger   3 = middle finger   2 = index finger   1 = thumb

Chord Spelling

1st (A), 3rd (C♯), 5th (E), ♭7th (G),
9th (B), 11th (D), 13th (F♯)

A13

Dominant 13th

(**Right** Hand)

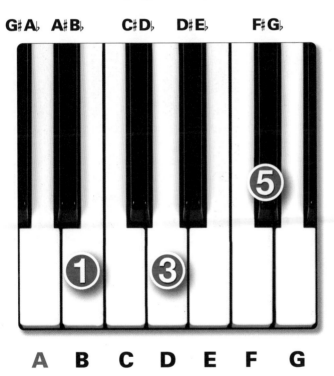

G#A♭ A#B♭   C#D♭   D#E♭   F#G♭

A   B   C   D   E   F   G

1 = thumb 2 = index finger 3 = middle finger 4 = ring finger 5 = little finger

A

B♭/A#

B

C

C#/D♭

D

E♭/D#

E

F

F#/G♭

G

A♭/G#

Other Chords

Chord Spelling

1st (A), 3rd (C#), 5th (E), ♭7th (G),
9th (B), 11th (D), 13th (F#)

B♭maj6/9

Major 6th add 9th

(**Left** Hand)

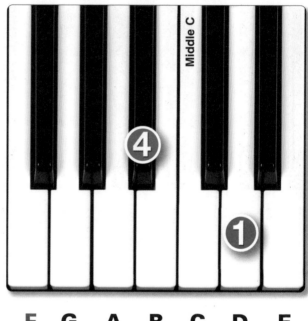

5 = little finger   4 = ring finger   3 = middle finger   2 = index finger   1 = thumb

Chord Spelling

1st (B♭), 3rd (D), 5th (F), 6th (G), 9th (C)

B♭maj6/9

Major 6th add 9th

(Right Hand)

F#G♭   G#A♭   A#B♭   C#D♭   D#E♭

F   G   A   B   C   D   E

1 = thumb   2 = index finger   3 = middle finger   4 = ring finger   5 = little finger

Chord Spelling

1st (B♭), 3rd (D), 5th (F), 6th (G), 9th (C)

A

B♭/A#

B

C

C#/D♭

D

E♭/D#

E

F

F#/G♭

G

A♭/G#

Other Chords

B♭m6/9

Minor 6th add 9th

(**Left** Hand)

F#G♭ G#A♭ A#B♭   C#D♭   D#E♭

Middle C

④   ②

F   G   A   B   C   D   E

5 = little finger   4 = ring finger   3 = middle finger   2 = index finger   1 = thumb

Chord Spelling

1st (B♭), ♭3rd (D♭), 5th (F), 6th (G), 9th (C)

B♭m6/9

Minor 6th add 9th

(**Right** Hand)

F#G♭ G#A♭ A#B♭   C#D♭   D#E♭

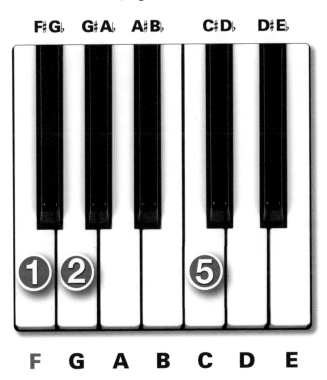

F G A B C D E

1 = thumb   2 = index finger   3 = middle finger   4 = ring finger   5 = little finger

Chord Spelling

1st (B♭), ♭3rd (D♭), 5th (F), 6th (G), 9th (C)

A

B♭/A#

B

C

C#/D♭

D

E♭/D#

E

F

F#/G♭

G

A♭/G#

Other Chords

A
Bb/A#
B
C
C#/Db
D
Eb/D#
E
F
F#/Gb
G
Ab/G#
Other
Chords

Bb6sus4

6th Suspended 4th

(**Left** Hand)

C#Db   D#Eb   F#Gb   G#Ab   A#Bb

C   D   E   F   G   A   B

5 = little finger   4 = ring finger   3 = middle finger   2 = index finger   1 = thumb

Chord Spelling

1st (Bb), 4th (Eb), 5th (F), 6th (G)

Bb6sus4

6th Suspended 4th

(**Right** Hand)

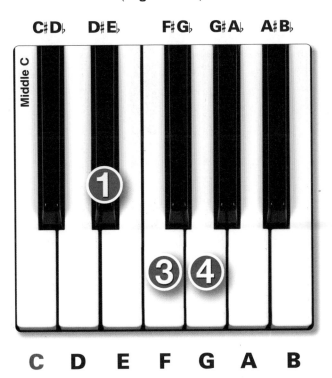

1 = thumb   2 = index finger   3 = middle finger   4 = ring finger   5 = little finger

Chord Spelling

1st (Bb), 4th (Eb), 5th (F), 6th (G)

A

Bb/A#

B

C

C#/Db

D

Eb/D#

E

F

F#/Gb

G

Ab/G#

Other Chords

B♭maj7+5

Major 7th Augmented 5th

(**Left** Hand)

C#D♭   D#E♭   F#G♭   G#A♭   A#B♭

C   D   E   F   G   A   B

5 = little finger   4 = ring finger   3 = middle finger   2 = index finger   1 = thumb

Chord Spelling

1st (B♭), 3rd (D), #5th (F#), 7th (A)

A
B♭/A#
B
C
C#/D♭
D
E♭/D#
E
F
F#/G♭
G
A♭/G#
Other Chords

B♭maj7+5

Major 7th Augmented 5th

(**Right** Hand)

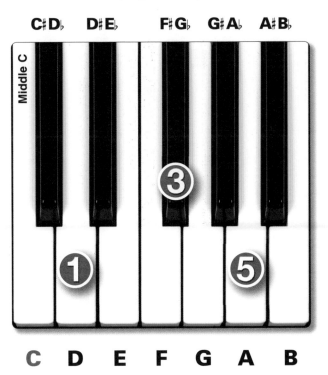

C♯D♭ D♯E♭ F♯G♭ G♯A♭ A♯B♭

Middle C

C D E F G A B

1 = thumb 2 = index finger 3 = middle finger 4 = ring finger 5 = little finger

A
B♭/A♯
B
C
C♯/D♭
D
E♭/D♯
E
F
F♯/G♭
G
A♭/G♯
Other Chords

Chord Spelling

1st (B♭), 3rd (D), ♯5th (F♯), 7th (A)

A
B♭/A♯
B
C
C♯/D♭
D
E♭/D♯
E
F
F♯/G♭
G
A♭/G♯
Other
Chords

B♭maj7sus4

Major 7th Suspended 4th

(**Left** Hand)

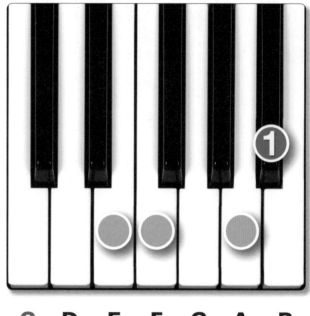

5 = little finger   4 = ring finger   3 = middle finger   2 = index finger   1 = thumb

Chord Spelling

1st (B♭), 4th (E), 5th (F), 7th (A)

B♭maj7sus4

Major 7th Suspended 4th

(**Right** Hand)

A

B♭/A#

B

C

C#/D♭

D

E♭/D#

E

F

F#/G♭

G

A♭/G#

Other Chords

C#D♭   D#E♭   F#G♭   G#A♭   A#B♭

Middle C

① ② ④

C D E F G A B

1 = thumb   2 = index finger   3 = middle finger   4 = ring finger   5 = little finger

Chord Spelling

1st (B♭), 4th (E♭), 5th (F), 7th (A)

B♭m-maj7

Minor-Major 7th

(**Left** Hand)

5 = little finger   4 = ring finger   3 = middle finger   2 = index finger   1 = thumb

Chord Spelling

1st (B♭), ♭3rd (D♭), 5th (F), 7th (A)

B♭m-maj7

Minor-Major 7th

(**Right** Hand)

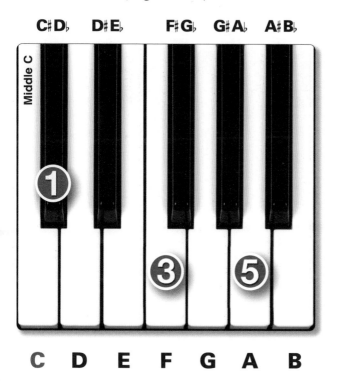

1 = thumb   2 = index finger   3 = middle finger   4 = ring finger   5 = little finger

Chord Spelling

1st (B♭), ♭3rd (D♭), 5th (F), 7th (A)

A

B♭/A♯

B

C

C♯/D♭

D

E♭/D♯

E

F

F♯/G♭

G

A♭/G♯

Other Chords

B♭maj9

Major 9th

(**Left** Hand)

F♯G♭   G♯A♭   A♯B♭   C♯D♭   D♯E♭

Middle C

② ... ... ① ...

F   G   A   B   C   D   E

5 = little finger   4 = ring finger   3 = middle finger   2 = index finger   1 = thumb

Chord Spelling

1st (B♭), 3rd (D), 5th (F), 7th (A), 9th (C)

A
B♭/A♯
B
C
C♯/D♭
D
E♭/D♯
E
F
F♯/G♭
G
A♭/G♯
Other Chords

B♭maj9
Major 9th
(**Right** Hand)

A
B♭/A♯
B
C
C♯/D♭
D
E♭/D♯
E
F
F♯/G♭
G
A♭/G♯
Other Chords

F♯G♭   G♯A♭   A♯B♭   C♯D♭   D♯E♭

①   **③**   **⑤**

F   G   A   B   C   D   E

1 = thumb   2 = index finger   3 = middle finger   4 = ring finger   5 = little finger

Chord Spelling

1st (B♭), 3rd (D), 5th (F), 7th (A), 9th (C)

A

Bb/A#

B

C

C#/Db

D

Eb/D#

E

F

F#/Gb

G

Ab/G#

Other
Chords

B♭m9

Minor 9th

(**Left** Hand)

5 = little finger   4 = ring finger   3 = middle finger   2 = index finger   1 = thumb

Chord Spelling

1st (B♭), ♭3rd (D♭), 5th (F), ♭7th (A♭), 9th (C)

B♭m9

Minor 9th

(**Right** Hand)

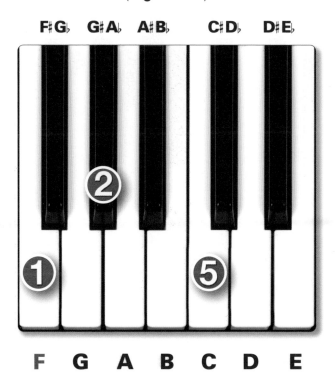

F#G♭   G#A♭   A#B♭   C#D♭   D#E♭

F   G   A   B   C   D   E

A

B♭/A#

B

C

C#/D♭

D

E♭/D#

E

F

F#/G♭

G

A♭/G#

Other Chords

1 = thumb   2 = index finger   3 = middle finger   4 = ring finger   5 = little finger

Chord Spelling

1st (B♭), ♭3rd (D♭), 5th (F), ♭7th (A♭), 9th (C)

B♭m-maj9

Minor-Major 9th

(**Left** Hand)

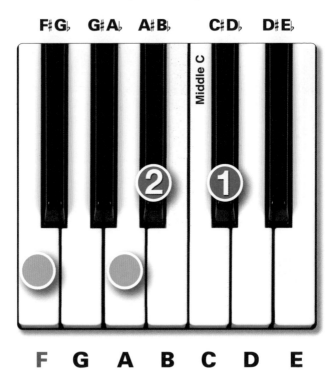

5 = little finger   4 = ring finger   3 = middle finger   2 = index finger   1 = thumb

Chord Spelling

1st (B♭), ♭3rd (D♭), 5th (F), 7th (A), 9th (C)

A

B♭/A♯

B

C

C♯/D♭

D

E♭/D♯

E

F

F♯/G♭

G

A♭/G♯

Other Chords

B♭m-maj9

Minor-Major 9th

(**Right** Hand)

A

B♭/A♯

B

C

C♯/D♭

D

E♭/D♯

E

F

F♯/G♭

G

A♭/G♯

Other Chords

F♯G♭   G♯A♭   A♯B♭   C♯D♭   D♯E♭

F   G   A   B   C   D   E

1 = thumb   2 = index finger   3 = middle finger   4 = ring finger   5 = little finger

Chord Spelling

1st (B♭), ♭3rd (D♭), 5th (F), 7th (A), 9th (C)

B♭maj11

Major 11th

(**Left** Hand)

F#G♭ G#A♭ A#B♭ C#D♭ D#E♭

Middle C

③

①

F G A B C D E

5 = little finger   4 = ring finger   3 = middle finger   2 = index finger   1 = thumb

Chord Spelling

1st (B♭), 3rd (D), 5th (F), 7th (A),
9th (C), 11th (E♭)

A

B♭/A#

B

C

C#/D♭

D

E♭/D#

E

F

F#/G♭

G

A♭/G#

Other
Chords

B♭maj11

Major 11th

(**Right** Hand)

F♯G♭   G♯A♭   A♯B♭   C♯D♭   D♯E♭

F   G   A   B   C   D   E

1 = thumb   2 = index finger   3 = middle finger   4 = ring finger   5 = little finger

Chord Spelling

1st (B♭), 3rd (D), 5th (F), 7th (A),
9th (C), 11th (E♭)

A

B♭/A♯

B

C

C♯/D♭

D

E♭/D♯

E

F

F♯/G♭

G

A♭/G♯

Other
Chords

B♭m11

Minor 11th

(**Left** Hand)

F#G♭ G#A♭ A#B♭ C#D♭ D#E♭

Middle C

F G A B C D E

5 = little finger   4 = ring finger   3 = middle finger   2 = index finger   1 = thumb

Chord Spelling

1st (B♭), ♭3rd (D♭), 5th (F), ♭7th (A♭),
9th (C), 11th (E♭)

B♭m11

Minor 11th

(**Right** Hand)

A

B♭/A♯

B

C

C♯/D♭

D

E♭/D♯

E

F

F♯/G♭

G

A♭/G♯

Other Chords

F♯G♭   G♯A♭   A♯B♭   C♯D♭   D♯E♭

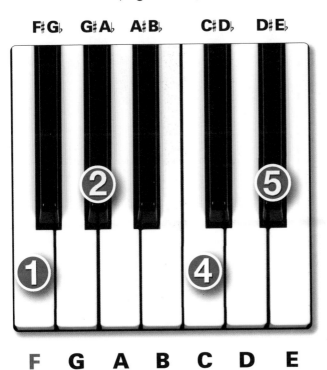

F   G   A   B   C   D   E

1 = thumb 2 = index finger 3 = middle finger 4 = ring finger 5 = little finger

Chord Spelling

1st (B♭), ♭3rd (D♭), 5th (F), ♭7th (A♭),
9th (C), 11th (E♭)

B♭11

Dominant 11th

(**Left** Hand)

A

B♭/A#

B

C

C#/D♭

D

E♭/D#

E

F

F#/G♭

G

A♭/G#

Other Chords

F#G♭ G#A♭ A#B♭   C#D♭ D#E♭

Middle C

③   ③   ①

F G A B C D E

5 = little finger 4 = ring finger 3 = middle finger 2 = index finger 1 = thumb

Chord Spelling

1st (B♭), 3rd (D), 5th (F), ♭7th (A♭),
9th (C), 11th (E♭)

B♭11

Dominant 11th

(**Right** Hand)

A

B♭/A♯

B

C

C♯/D♭

D

E♭/D♯

E

F

F♯/G♭

G

A♭/G♯

Other Chords

F♯G♭ G♯A♭ A♯B♭   C♯D♭ D♯E♭

F G A B C D E

1 = thumb 2 = index finger 3 = middle finger 4 = ring finger 5 = little finger

Chord Spelling

1st (B♭), 3rd (D), 5th (F), ♭7th (A♭),
9th (C), 11th (E♭)

B♭maj13
Major 13th
(**Left** Hand)

G♯A♭ A♯B♭   C♯D♭   D♯E♭   F♯G♭

Middle C

⑤

③   ①

A   B   C   D   E   F   G

5 = little finger   4 = ring finger   3 = middle finger   2 = index finger   1 = thumb

A
B♭/A♯
B
C
C♯/D♭
D
E♭/D♯
E
F
F♯/G♭
G
A♭/G♯
Other Chords

Chord Spelling

1st (B♭), 3rd (D), 5th (F), 7th (A),
9th (C), 11th (E♭), 13th (G)

B♭maj13

Major 13th

(**Right** Hand)

A

B♭/A♯

B

C

C♯/D♭

D

E♭/D♯

E

F

F♯/G♭

G

A♭/G♯

Other Chords

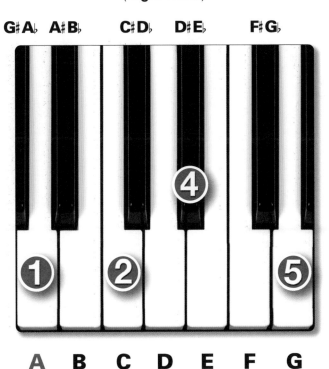

G♯A♭   A♯B♭   C♯D♭   D♯E♭   F♯G♭

A   B   C   D   E   F   G

1 = thumb   2 = index finger   3 = middle finger   4 = ring finger   5 = little finger

Chord Spelling

1st (B♭), 3rd (D), 5th (F), 7th (A),
9th (C), 11th (E♭), 13th (G)

A

B♭/A♯

B

C

C♯/D♭

D

E♭/D♯

E

F

F♯/G♭

G

A♭/G♯

Other
Chords

B♭m13

Minor 13th

(**Left** Hand)

G♯A♭ A♯B♭   C♯D♭   D♯E♭   F♯G♭

Middle C

⑤   ④   ①

A   B   C   D   E   F   G

5 = little finger   4 = ring finger   3 = middle finger   2 = index finger   1 = thumb

Chord Spelling

1st (B♭), ♭3rd (D♭), 5th (F), ♭7th (A♭),
9th (C), 11th (E♭), 13th (G)

B♭m13

Minor 13th

(**Right** Hand)

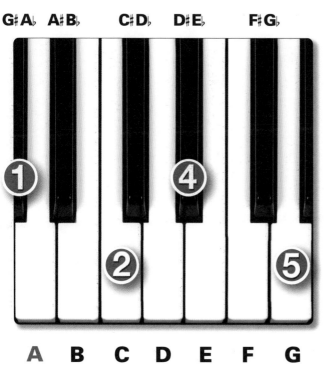

G♯A♭ A♯B♭ C♯D♭ D♯E♭ F♯G♭

A B C D E F G

1 = thumb   2 = index finger   3 = middle finger   4 = ring finger   5 = little finger

Chord Spelling

1st (B♭), ♭3rd (D♭), 5th (F), ♭7th (A♭),
9th (C), 11th (E♭), 13th (G)

A

B♭/A♯

B

C

C♯/D♭

D

E♭/D♯

E

F

F♯/G♭

G

A♭/G♯

Other Chords

A

B♭/A♯

B

C

C♯/D♭

D

E♭/D♯

E

F

F♯/G♭

G

A♭/G♯

Other
Chords

B♭13

Dominant 13th

(**Left** Hand)

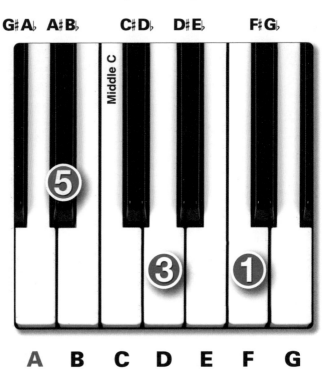

G♯A♭ A♯B♭   C♯D♭   D♯E♭   F♯G♭

Middle C

A   B   C   D   E   F   G

5 = little finger   4 = ring finger   3 = middle finger   2 = index finger   1 = thumb

Chord Spelling

1st (B♭), 3rd (D), 5th (F), ♭7th (A♭),
9th (C), 11th (E♭), 13th (G)

B♭13

Dominant 13th

(**Right** Hand)

A

B♭/A♯

B

C

C♯/D♭

D

E♭/D♯

E

F

F♯/G♭

G

A♭/G♯

Other Chords

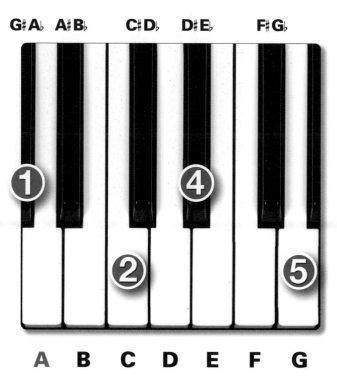

G♯A♭ A♯B♭   C♯D♭   D♯E♭   F♯G♭

A B C D E F G

1 = thumb   2 = index finger   3 = middle finger   4 = ring finger   5 = little finger

Chord Spelling

1st (B♭), 3rd (D), 5th (F), ♭7th (A♭),
9th (C), 11th (E♭), 13th (G)

Bmaj6/9
Major 6th add 9th
(**Left** Hand)

5 = little finger   4 = ring finger   3 = middle finger   2 = index finger   1 = thumb

Chord Spelling

1st (B), 3rd (D♯), 5th (F♯), 6th (G♯), 9th (C♯)

Bmaj6/9

Major 6th add 9th

(**Right** Hand)

F#G♭   G#A♭   A#B♭   C#D♭   D#E♭

F   G   A   B   C   D   E

A
B♭/A#
B
C
C#/D♭
D
E♭/D#
E
F
F#/G♭
G
A♭/G#
Other Chords

1 = thumb   2 = index finger   3 = middle finger   4 = ring finger   5 = little finger

Chord Spelling

1st (B), 3rd (D#), 5th (F#), 6th (G#), 9th (C#)

Bm6/9

Minor 6th add 9th

(**Left** Hand)

F#G♭   G#A♭   A#B♭   C#D♭   D#E♭

Middle C

F   G   A   B   C   D   E

5 = little finger   4 = ring finger   3 = middle finger   2 = index finger   1 = thumb

Chord Spelling

1st (B), ♭3rd (D), 5th (F#), 6th (G#), 9th (C#)

A

B♭/A#

B

C

C#/D♭

D

E♭/D#

E

F

F#/G♭

G

A♭/G#

Other
Chords

Bm6/9

Minor 6th add 9th

(**Right** Hand)

F#G♭ G#A♭ A#B♭   C#D♭   D#E♭

F G A B C D E

1 = thumb 2 = index finger 3 = middle finger 4 = ring finger 5 = little finger

Chord Spelling

1st (B), ♭3rd (D), 5th (F#), 6th (G#), 9th (C#)

A

B♭/A#

B

C

C#/D♭

D

E♭/D#

E

F

F#/G♭

G

A♭/G#

Other
Chords

B6sus4

6th Suspended 4th

(**Left** Hand)

C#D♭   D#E♭   F#G♭   G#A♭   A#B♭

C   D   E   F   G   A   B

5 = little finger   4 = ring finger   3 = middle finger   2 = index finger   1 = thumb

Chord Spelling

1st (B), 4th (E), 5th (F#), 6th (G#)

A
B♭/A#
B
C
C#/D♭
D
E♭/D#
E
F
F#/G♭
G
A♭/G#
Other Chords

B6sus4

6th Suspended 4th

(**Right** Hand)

C#D♭ D#E♭ F#G♭ G#A♭ A#B♭

C D E F G A B

1 = thumb   2 = index finger   3 = middle finger   4 = ring finger   5 = little finger

Chord Spelling

1st (B), 4th (E), 5th (F#), 6th (G#)

A

B♭/A#

B

C

C#/D♭

D

E♭/D#

E

F

F#/G♭

G

A♭/G#

Other Chords

Bmaj7+5

Major 7th Augmented 5th

(**Left** Hand)

5 = little finger   4 = ring finger   3 = middle finger   2 = index finger   1 = thumb

Chord Spelling

1st (B), 3rd (D♯), ♯5th (Fx), 7th (A♯)

Bmaj7+5

Major 7th Augmented 5th

(**Right** Hand)

A

Bb/A#

B

C

C#/Db

D

Eb/D#

E

F

F#/Gb

G

Ab/G#

Other Chords

C#Db   D#Eb   F#Gb   G#Ab   A#Bb

Middle C

C   D   E   F   G   A   B

1 = thumb   2 = index finger   3 = middle finger   4 = ring finger   5 = little finger

Chord Spelling

1st (B), 3rd (D#), #5th (Fx), 7th (A#)

Bmaj7sus4
Major 7th Suspended 4th

(**Left** Hand)

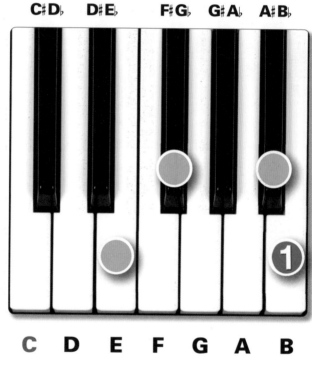

C#D♭ D#E♭ F#G♭ G#A♭ A#B♭

C D E F G A B

5 = little finger 4 = ring finger 3 = middle finger 2 = index finger 1 = thumb

Chord Spelling

1st (B), 4th (E), 5th (F#), 7th (A#)

Bmaj7sus4

Major 7th Suspended 4th

(**Right** Hand)

A

B♭/A♯

B

C

C♯/D♭

D

E♭/D♯

E

F

F♯/G♭

G

A♭/G♯

Other Chords

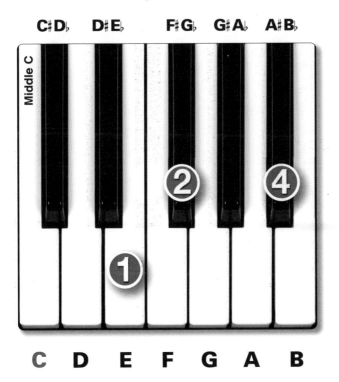

C♯D♭   D♯E♭   F♯G♭   G♯A♭   A♯B♭

Middle C

C   D   E   F   G   A   B

1 = thumb   2 = index finger   3 = middle finger   4 = ring finger   5 = little finger

Chord Spelling

1st (B), 4th (E), 5th (F♯), 7th (A♯)

Bm-maj7
Minor-Major 7th

(**Left** Hand)

C#D♭   D#E♭   F#G♭ G#A♭ A#B♭

C   D   E   F   G   A   B

5 = little finger **4** = ring finger **3** = middle finger **2** = index finger **1** = thumb

Chord Spelling
1st (B), ♭3rd (D), 5th (F#), 7th (A#)

Bm-maj7
Minor-Major 7th
(**Right** Hand)

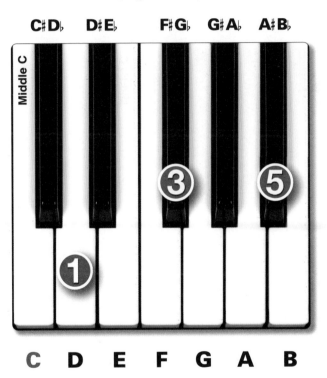

A
Bb/A#
B
C
C#/Db
D
Eb/D#
E
F
F#/Gb
G
Ab/G#
Other Chords

1 = thumb   2 = index finger   3 = middle finger   4 = ring finger   5 = little finger

Chord Spelling

1st (B), b3rd (D), 5th (F#), 7th (A#)

Bmaj9

Major 9th

(**Left** Hand)

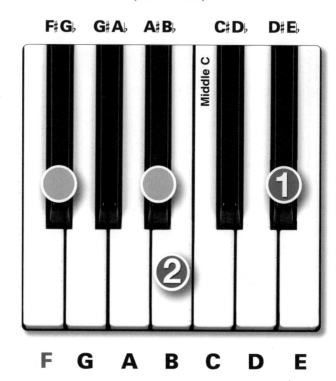

5 = little finger   4 = ring finger   3 = middle finger   2 = index finger   1 = thumb

Chord Spelling

1st (B), 3rd (D♯), 5th (F♯), 7th (A♯), 9th (C♯)

Bmaj9

Major 9th

(**Right** Hand)

A

B♭/A♯

B

C

C♯/D♭

D

E♭/D♯

E

F

F♯/G♭

G

A♭/G♯

Other Chords

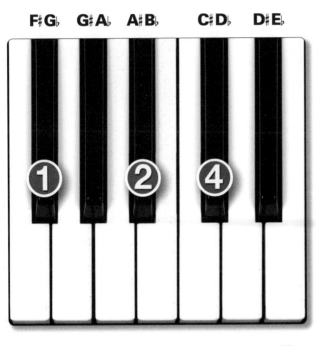

F♯G♭   G♯A♭   A♯B♭   C♯D♭   D♯E♭

F   G   A   B   C   D   E

1 = thumb   2 = index finger   3 = middle finger   4 = ring finger   5 = little finger

Chord Spelling

1st (B), 3rd (D♯), 5th (F♯), 7th (A♯), 9th (C♯)

Bm9

Minor 9th

(**Left** Hand)

5 = little finger   4 = ring finger   3 = middle finger   2 = index finger   1 = thumb

Chord Spelling

1st (B), ♭3rd (D), 5th (F#), ♭7th (A), 9th (C#)

Bm9

Minor 9th

(**Right** Hand)

1 = thumb 2 = index finger 3 = middle finger 4 = ring finger 5 = little finger

Chord Spelling

1st (B), ♭3rd (D), 5th (F♯), ♭7th (A), 9th (C♯)

A

B♭/A♯

B

C

C♯/D♭

D

E♭/D♯

E

F

F♯/G♭

G

A♭/G♯

Other Chords

Bm-maj9
Minor-Major 9th

(**Left** Hand)

5 = little finger   4 = ring finger   3 = middle finger   2 = index finger   1 = thumb

Chord Spelling

1st (B), ♭3rd (D), 5th (F♯), 7th (A♯), 9th (C♯)

Bm-maj9

Minor-Major 9th

(**Right** Hand)

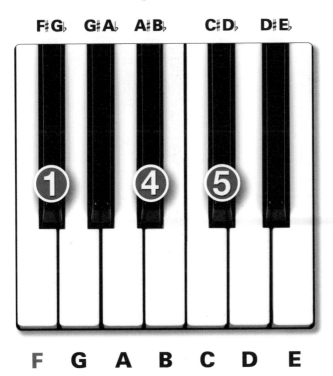

F#G♭   G#A♭   A#B♭   C#D♭   D#E♭

F   G   A   B   C   D   E

A
B♭/A#
B
C
C#/D♭
D
E♭/D#
E
F
F#/G♭
G
A♭/G#
Other Chords

1 = thumb   2 = index finger   3 = middle finger   4 = ring finger   5 = little finger

Chord Spelling

1st (B), ♭3rd (D), 5th (F#), 7th (A#), 9th (C#)

Bmaj11
Major 11th
(**Left** Hand)

5 = little finger   4 = ring finger   3 = middle finger   2 = index finger   1 = thumb

Chord Spelling

1st (B), 3rd (D#), 5th (F#), 7th (A#),
9th (C#), 11th (E)

Bmaj11

Major 11th

(**Right** Hand)

A

B♭/A♯

B

C

C♯/D♭

D

E♭/D♯

E

F

F♯/G♭

G

A♭/G♯

Other Chords

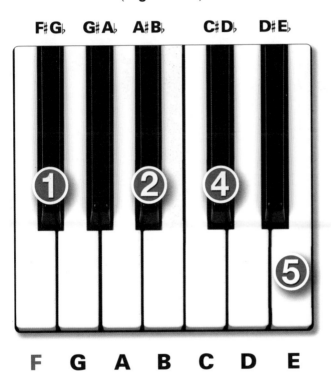

F#G♭ G#A♭ A#B♭   C#D♭   D#E♭

F G A B C D E

1 = thumb   2 = index finger   3 = middle finger   4 = ring finger   5 = little finger

Chord Spelling

1st (B), 3rd (D♯), 5th (F♯), 7th (A♯),
9th (C♯), 11th (E)

A

B♭/A♯

B

C

C♯/D♭

D

E♭/D♯

E

F

F♯/G♭

G

A♭/G♯

Other
Chords

Bm11
Minor 11th
(**Left** Hand)

F♯G♭ **G♯A♭** **A♯B♭** **C♯D♭** **D♯E♭**

Middle C

F   G   A   B   C   D   E

5 = little finger   4 = ring finger   3 = middle finger   2 = index finger   1 = thumb

Chord Spelling

1st (B), ♭3rd (D), 5th (F♯), ♭7th (A),
9th (C♯), 11th (E)

Bm11
Minor 11th

(**Right** Hand)

A
Bb/A#
B
C
C#/Db
D
Eb/D#
E
F
F#/Gb
G
Ab/G#
Other Chords

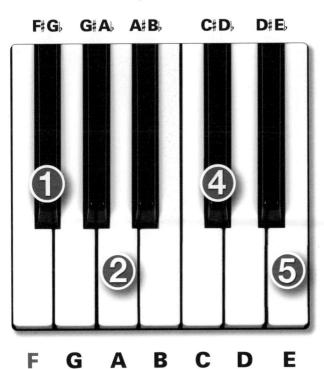

F#Gb   G#Ab   A#Bb   C#Db   D#Eb

F   G   A   B   C   D   E

1 = thumb   2 = index finger   3 = middle finger   4 = ring finger   5 = little finger

Chord Spelling

1st (B), b3rd (D), 5th (F#), b7th (A),
9th (C#), 11th (E)

B11

Dominant 11th

(**Left** Hand)

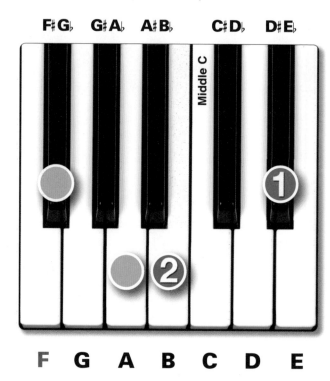

5 = little finger 4 = ring finger 3 = middle finger 2 = index finger 1 = thumb

Chord Spelling

1st (B), 3rd (D#), 5th (F#), ♭7th (A),
9th (C#), 11th (E)

B11

Dominant 11th

(**Right** Hand)

A
B♭/A♯
B
C
C♯/D♭
D
E♭/D♯
E
F
F♯/G♭
G
A♭/G♯
Other Chords

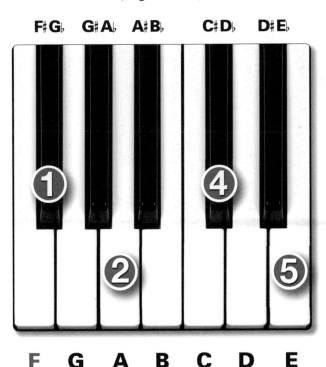

F♯G♭   G♯A♭   A♯B♭   C♯D♭   D♯E♭

F   G   A   B   C   D   E

1 = thumb   2 = index finger   3 = middle finger   4 = ring finger   5 = little finger

Chord Spelling

1st (B), 3rd (D♯), 5th (F♯), ♭7th (A),
9th (C♯), 11th (E)

Bmaj13
Major 13th
(**Left** Hand)

A#B♭   C#D♭   D#E♭   F#G♭   G#A♭

A B C D E F G

5 = little finger   4 = ring finger   3 = middle finger   2 = index finger   1 = thumb

Chord Spelling

1st (B), 3rd (D#), 5th (F#), 7th (A#),
9th (C#), 11th (E), 13th (G#)

Bmaj13
Major 13th

(**Right** Hand)

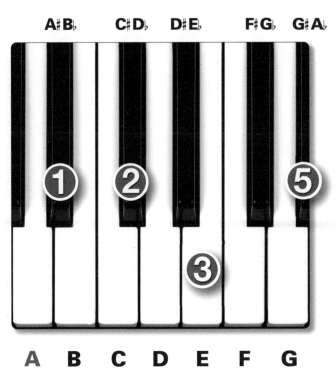

A#B♭   C#D♭   D#E♭   F#G♭   G#A♭

A B C D E F G

A
B♭/A#
B
C
C#/D♭
D
E♭/D#
E
F
F#/G♭
G
A♭/G#
Other Chords

1 = thumb   2 = index finger   3 = middle finger   4 = ring finger   5 = little finger

Chord Spelling

1st (B), 3rd (D#), 5th (F#), 7th (A#),
9th (C#), 11th (E), 13th (G#)

Bm13

Minor 13th

(**Left** Hand)

A#B♭ C#D♭ D#E♭ F#G♭ G#A♭

Middle C

① ⑤ ③

A B C D E F G

5 = little finger   4 = ring finger   3 = middle finger   2 = index finger   1 = thumb

Chord Spelling

1st (B), ♭3rd (D), 5th (F♯), ♭7th (A),
9th (C♯), 11th (E), 13th (G♯)

Bm13
Minor 13th

(**Right** Hand)

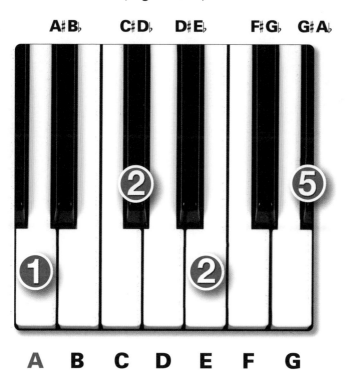

A♯B♭   C♯D♭   D♯E♭   F♯G♭   G♯A♭

A B C D E F G

1 = thumb 2 = index finger 3 = middle finger 4 = ring finger 5 = little finger

Chord Spelling

1st (B), ♭3rd (D), 5th (F♯), ♭7th (A),
9th (C♯), 11th (E), 13th (G♯)

A

B♭/A♯

B

C

C♯/D♭

D

E♭/D♯

E

F

F♯/G♭

G

A♭/G♯

Other Chords

B13

Dominant 13th

(**Left** Hand)

A#B♭   C#D♭   D#E♭   F#G♭   G#A♭

Middle C

③   ①

⑤

A   B   C   D   E   F   G

5 = little finger   4 = ring finger   3 = middle finger   2 = index finger   1 = thumb

A
B♭/A#
B
C
C#/D♭
D
E♭/D#
E
F
F#/G♭
G
A♭/G#
Other Chords

Chord Spelling

1st (B), 3rd (D#), 5th (F#), ♭7th (A),
9th (C#), 11th (E), 13th (G#)

B13

Dominant 13th

(**Right** Hand)

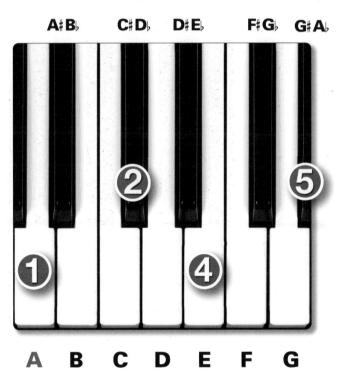

A#B♭　　C#D♭　D#E♭　　F#G♭　G#A♭

A　B　C　D　E　F　G

1 = thumb　2 = index finger　3 = middle finger　4 = ring finger　5 = little finger

Chord Spelling

1st (B), 3rd (D#), 5th (F#), ♭7th (A),
9th (C#), 11th (E), 13th (G#)

A

B♭/A#

B

C

C#/D♭

D

E♭/D#

E

F

F#/G♭

G

A♭/G#

Other
Chords

Cmaj6/9

Major 6th add 9th

(**Left** Hand)

F#G♭ G#A♭ A#B♭ C#D♭ D#E♭

Middle C

F G A B C D E

5 = little finger   4 = ring finger   3 = middle finger   2 = index finger   1 = thumb

Chord Spelling

1st (C), 3rd (E), 5th (G), 6th (A), 9th (D)

A
B♭/A#
B
C
C#/D♭
D
E♭/D#
E
F
F#/G♭
G
A♭/G#
Other Chords

Cmaj6/9
Major 6th add 9th

(**Right** Hand)

F♯G♭ G♯A♭ A♯B♭   C♯D♭   D♯E♭

F   G   A   B   C   D   E

1 = thumb   2 = index finger   3 = middle finger   4 = ring finger   5 = little finger

Chord Spelling

1st (C), 3rd (E), 5th (G), 6th (A), 9th (D)

A

B♭/A♯

B

C

C♯/D♭

D

E♭/D♯

E

F

F♯/G♭

G

A♭/G♯

Other
Chords

Cm6/9

Minor 6th add 9th

(**Left** Hand)

F#G♭   G#A♭   A#B♭   C#D♭   D#E♭

Middle C

⑤

③

F   G   A   B   C   D   E

5 = little finger   4 = ring finger   3 = middle finger   2 = index finger   1 = thumb

Chord Spelling

1st (C), ♭3rd (E♭), 5th (G), 6th (A), 9th (D)

A

B♭/A#

B

C

C#/D♭

D

E♭/D#

E

F

F#/G♭

G

A♭/G#

Other
Chords

Cm6/9

Minor 6th add 9th

(**Right** Hand)

F#G♭   G#A♭   A#B♭   C#D♭   D#E♭

F   G   A   B   C   D   E

1 = thumb   2 = index finger   3 = middle finger   4 = ring finger   5 = little finger

Chord Spelling

1st (C), ♭3rd (E♭), 5th (G), 6th (A), 9th (D)

A

B♭/A#

B

C

C#/D♭

D

E♭/D#

E

F

F#/G♭

G

A♭/G#

Other Chords

C6sus4

6th Suspended 4th

(**Left** Hand)

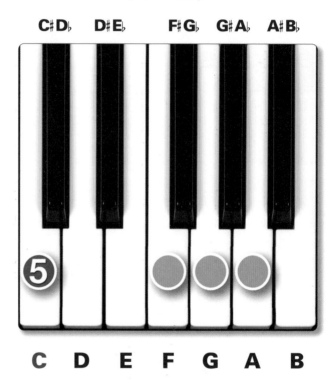

C#D♭   D#E♭   F#G♭   G#A♭   A#B♭

C   D   E   F   G   A   B

5 = little finger   4 = ring finger   3 = middle finger   2 = index finger   1 = thumb

Chord Spelling

1st (C), 4th (F), 5th (G), 6th (A)

A

B♭/A#

B

C

C#/D♭

D

E♭/D#

E

F

F#/G♭

G

A♭/G#

Other
Chords

C6sus4

6th Suspended 4th

(**Right** Hand)

A
Bb/A#
B
C
C#/Db
D
Eb/D#
E
F
F#/Gb
G
Ab/G#
Other Chords

1 = thumb   2 = index finger   3 = middle finger   4 = ring finger   5 = little finger

Chord Spelling

1st (C), 4th (F), 5th (G), 6th (A)

Cmaj7+5

Major 7th Augmented 5th

(**Left** Hand)

5 = little finger   4 = ring finger   3 = middle finger   2 = index finger   1 = thumb

Chord Spelling

1st (C), 3rd (E), #5th (G#), 7th (B)

Cmaj7+5

Major 7th Augmented 5th

(**Right** Hand)

A
B♭/A♯
B
C
C♯/D♭
D
E♭/D♯
E
F
F♯/G♭
G
A♭/G♯
Other Chords

C♯D♭   D♯E♭   F♯G♭   G♯A♭   A♯B♭

Middle C

① ② ④ ⑤

C   D   E   F   G   A   B

1 = thumb   2 = index finger   3 = middle finger   4 = ring finger   5 = little finger

Chord Spelling

1st (C), 3rd (E), ♯5th (G♯), 7th (B)

Cmaj7sus4

Major 7th Suspended 4th

(**Left** Hand)

C#D♭   D#E♭   F#G♭   G#A♭   A#B♭

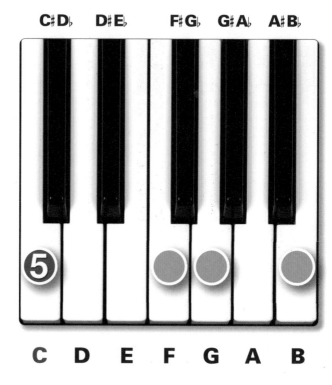

C   D   E   F   G   A   B

5 = little finger   4 = ring finger   3 = middle finger   2 = index finger   1 = thumb

Chord Spelling

1st (C), 4th (F), 5th (G), 7th (B)

A
B♭/A#
B
C
C#/D♭
D
E♭/D#
E
F
F#/G♭
G
A♭/G#
Other
Chords

Cmaj7sus4

Major 7th Suspended 4th

(**Right** Hand)

1 = thumb   2 = index finger   3 = middle finger   4 = ring finger   5 = little finger

Chord Spelling

1st (C), 4th (F), 5th (G), 7th (B)

A

B♭/A♯

B

C

C♯/D♭

D

E♭/D♯

E

F

F♯/G♭

G

A♭/G♯

Other Chords

Cm-maj7
Minor-Major 7th

(**Left** Hand)

C#D♭   D#E♭   F#G♭   G#A♭   A#B♭

C D E F G A B

5 = little finger   4 = ring finger   3 = middle finger   2 = index finger   1 = thumb

Chord Spelling

1st (C), ♭3rd (E♭), 5th (G), 7th (B)

Cm-maj7
Minor-Major 7th

(**Right** Hand)

A

B♭/A♯

B

C

C♯/D♭

D

E♭/D♯

E

F

F♯/G♭

G

A♭/G♯

Other Chords

1 = thumb   2 = index finger   3 = middle finger   4 = ring finger   5 = little finger

Chord Spelling
1st (C), ♭3rd (E♭), 5th (G), 7th (B)

Cmaj9

Major 9th

(**Left** Hand)

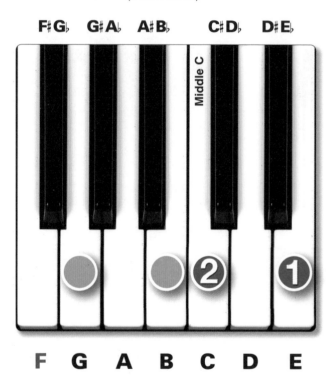

5 = little finger   4 = ring finger   3 = middle finger   2 = index finger   1 = thumb

Chord Spelling

1st (C), 3rd (E), 5th (G), 7th (B), 9th (D)

Cmaj9

Major 9th

(**Right** Hand)

F♯G♭   G♯A♭   A♯B♭   C♯D♭   D♯E♭

F   G   A   B   C   D   E

1 = thumb   2 = index finger   3 = middle finger   4 = ring finger   5 = little finger

Chord Spelling

1st (C), 3rd (E), 5th (G), 7th (B), 9th (D)

A

B♭/A♯

B

C

C♯/D♭

D

E♭/D♯

E

F

F♯/G♭

G

A♭/G♯

Other Chords

Cm9

Minor 9th

(**Left** Hand)

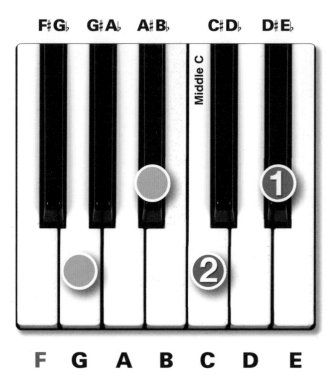

F#G♭   G#A♭   A#B♭   C#D♭   D#E♭

Middle C

F   G   A   B   C   D   E

5 = little finger   4 = ring finger   3 = middle finger   2 = index finger   1 = thumb

Chord Spelling

1st (C), ♭3rd (E♭), 5th (G), ♭7th (B♭), 9th (D)

Cm9

Minor 9th

(**Right** Hand)

F#G♭ G#A♭ A#B♭   C#D♭ D#E♭

F   G   A   B   C   D   E

A
B♭/A#
B
C
C#/D♭
D
E♭/D#
E
F
F#/G♭
G
A♭/G#
Other Chords

1 = thumb   2 = index finger   3 = middle finger   4 = ring finger   5 = little finger

Chord Spelling

1st (C), ♭3rd (E♭), 5th (G), ♭7th (B♭), 9th (D)

Cm-maj9

Minor-Major 9th

(**Left** Hand)

5 = little finger   4 = ring finger   3 = middle finger   2 = index finger   1 = thumb

Chord Spelling

1st (C), ♭3rd (E♭), 5th (G), 7th (B), 9th (D)

Cm-maj9
Minor-Major 9th
(**Right** Hand)

F#G♭   G#A♭   A#B♭   C#D♭   D#E♭

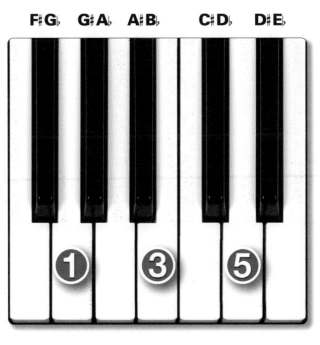

F   G   A   B   C   D   E

1 = thumb   2 = index finger   3 = middle finger   4 = ring finger   5 = little finger

Chord Spelling
1st (C), ♭3rd (E♭), 5th (G), 7th (B), 9th (D)

A

B♭/A#

B

C

C#/D♭

D

E♭/D#

E

F

F#/G♭

G

A♭/G#

Other Chords

Cmaj11

Major 11th

(**Left** Hand)

5 = little finger 4 = ring finger 3 = middle finger 2 = index finger 1 = thumb

Chord Spelling

1st (C), 3rd (E), 5th (G), 7th (B),
9th (D), 11th (F)

Cmaj11
Major 11th

(**Right** Hand)

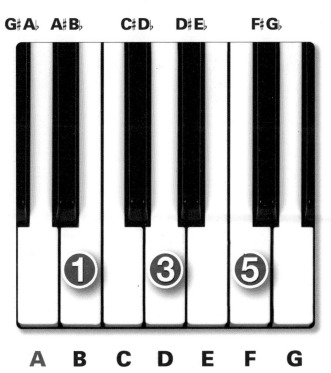

1 = thumb   2 = index finger   3 = middle finger   4 = ring finger   5 = little finger

Chord Spelling

1st (C), 3rd (E), 5th (G), 7th (B),
9th (D), 11th (F)

A
B♭/A♯
B
C
C♯/D♭
D
E♭/D♯
E
F
F♯/G♭
G
A♭/G♯
Other Chords

Cm11

Minor 11th

(**Left** Hand)

5 = little finger   4 = ring finger   3 = middle finger   2 = index finger   1 = thumb

Chord Spelling

1st (C), ♭3rd (E♭), 5th (G), ♭7th (B♭),
9th (D), 11th (F)

Cm11

Minor 11th

(**Right** Hand)

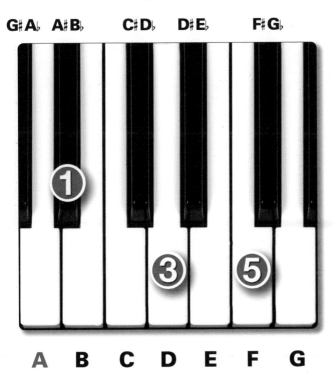

G#A♭   A#B♭   C#D♭   D#E♭   F#G♭

A   B   C   D   E   F   G

1 = thumb   2 = index finger   3 = middle finger   4 = ring finger   5 = little finger

Chord Spelling

1st (C), ♭3rd (E♭), 5th (G), ♭7th (B♭),
9th (D), 11th (F)

A

B♭/A#

B

C

C#/D♭

D

E♭/D#

E

F

F#/G♭

G

A♭/G#

Other Chords

A

B♭/A♯

B

C

C♯/D♭

D

E♭/D♯

E

F

F♯/G♭

G

A♭/G♯

Other Chords

C11

Dominant 11th

(**Left** Hand)

G♯A♭ **A♯B♭**   **C♯D♭**   **D♯E♭**   **F♯G♭**

Middle C

⑤ ③ ①

A **B** **C** **D** **E** **F** **G**

5 = little finger   4 = ring finger   3 = middle finger   2 = index finger   1 = thumb

Chord Spelling

1st (C), 3rd (E), 5th (G), ♭7th (B♭),
9th (D), 11th (F)

C11

Dominant 11th

(**Right** Hand)

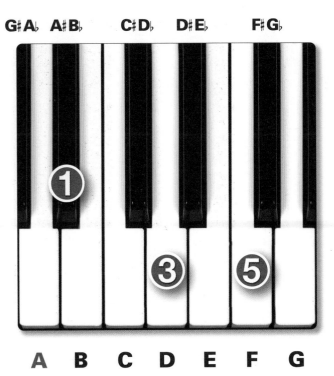

G#A♭ A#B♭   C#D♭   D#E♭   F#G♭

A   B   C   D   E   F   G

1 = thumb   2 = index finger   3 = middle finger   4 = ring finger   5 = little finger

A

B♭/A#

B

C

C#/D♭

D

E♭/D#

E

F

F#/G♭

G

A♭/G#

Other
Chords

Chord Spelling

1st (C), 3rd (E), 5th (G), ♭7th (B♭),
9th (D), 11th (F)

Cmaj13
Major 13th
(**Left** Hand)

C#D♭   D#E♭   F#G♭   G#A♭   A#B♭

C D E F G A B

5 = little finger   4 = ring finger   3 = middle finger   2 = index finger   1 = thumb

Chord Spelling

1st (C), 3rd (E), 5th (G), 7th (B),
9th (D), 11th (F), 13th (A)

A

B♭/A#

B

C

C#/D♭

D

E♭/D#

E

F

F#/G♭

G

A♭/G#

Other
Chords

Cmaj13
Major 13th
(**Right** Hand)

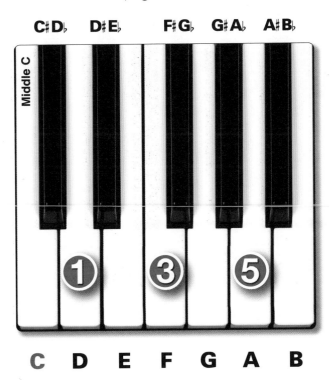

C#D♭   D#E♭   F#G♭   G#A♭   A#B♭

Middle C

① ③ ⑤

C D E F G A B

1 = thumb   2 = index finger   3 = middle finger   4 = ring finger   5 = little finger

Chord Spelling

1st (C), 3rd (E), 5th (G), 7th (B),
9th (D), 11th (F), 13th (A)

A
B♭/A#
B
C
C#/D♭
D
E♭/D#
E
F
F#/G♭
G
A♭/G#
Other Chords

Cm13

Minor 13th

(Left Hand)

C#D♭   D#E♭   F#G♭   G#A♭   A#B♭

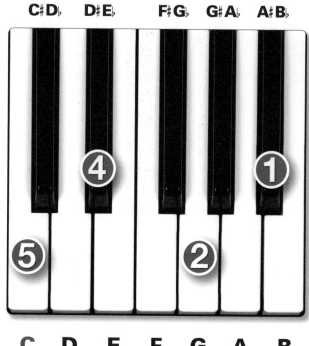

C   D   E   F   G   A   B

5 = little finger   4 = ring finger   3 = middle finger   2 = index finger   1 = thumb

Chord Spelling

1st (C), ♭3rd (E♭), 5th (G), ♭7th (B♭),
9th (D), 11th (F), 13th (A)

Cm13

Minor 13th

(**Right** Hand)

1 = thumb   2 = index finger   3 = middle finger   4 = ring finger   5 = little finger

Chord Spelling

1st (C), ♭3rd (E♭), 5th (G), ♭7th (B♭),
9th (D), 11th (F), 13th (A)

A
B♭/A♯
B
C
C♯/D♭
D
E♭/D♯
E
F
F♯/G♭
G
A♭/G♯
Other Chords

C13

Dominant 13th

(**Left** Hand)

C#D♭   D#E♭   F#G♭   G#A♭   A#B♭

C   D   E   F   G   A   B

5 = little finger   4 = ring finger   3 = middle finger   2 = index finger   1 = thumb

Chord Spelling

1st (C), 3rd (E), 5th (G), ♭7th (B♭),
9th (D), 11th (F), 13th (A)

A
B♭/A#
B
C
C#/D♭
D
E♭/D#
E
F
F#/G♭
G
A♭/G#
Other
Chords

C13

Dominant 13th

(**Right** Hand)

A
Bb/A#
B
C
C#/Db
D
Eb/D#
E
F
F#/Gb
G
Ab/G#
Other Chords

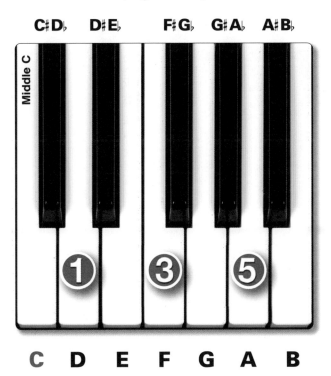

1 = thumb   2 = index finger   3 = middle finger   4 = ring finger   5 = little finger

Chord Spelling

1st (C), 3rd (E), 5th (G), b7th (Bb),
9th (D), 11th (F), 13th (A)

A

B♭/A♯

B

C

C♯/D♭

D

E♭/D♯

E

F

F♯/G♭

G

A♭/G♯

Other
Chords

C♯maj6/9

Major 6th add 9th

(**Left** Hand)

F♯G♭　G♯A♭　A♯B♭　　C♯D♭　D♯E♭

Middle C

F　G　A　B　C　D　E

5 = little finger   4 = ring finger   3 = middle finger   2 = index finger   1 = thumb

Chord Spelling

1st (C♯), 3rd (E♯), 5th (G♯), 6th (A♯), 9th (D♯)

C#maj6/9
Major 6th add 9th

(**Right** Hand)

F#G♭ G#A♭ A#B♭   C#D♭   D#E♭

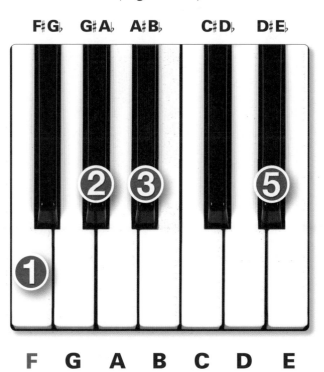

F   G   A   B   C   D   E

1 = thumb   2 = index finger   3 = middle finger   4 = ring finger   5 = little finger

Chord Spelling

1st (C#), 3rd (E#), 5th (G#), 6th (A#), 9th (D#)

A
B♭/A#
B
C
C#/D♭
D
E♭/D#
E
F
F#/G♭
G
A♭/G#
Other Chords

C#m6/9

Minor 6th add 9th

(**Left** Hand)

F#G♭   G#A♭   A#B♭   C#D♭   D#E♭

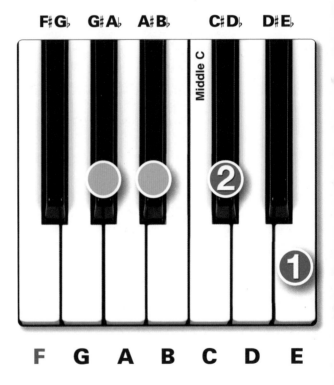

F   G   A   B   C   D   E

5 = little finger   4 = ring finger   3 = middle finger   2 = index finger   1 = thumb

Chord Spelling

1st (C#), ♭3rd (E), 5th (G#), 6th (A#), 9th (D#)

C#m6/9

Minor 6th add 9th

(**Right** Hand)

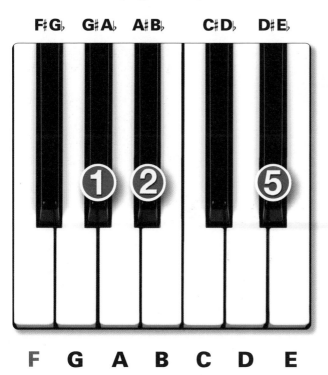

F#G♭   G#A♭   A#B♭   C#D♭   D#E♭

F   G   A   B   C   D   E

1 = thumb   2 = index finger   3 = middle finger   4 = ring finger   5 = little finger

Chord Spelling

1st (C#), ♭3rd (E), 5th (G#), 6th (A#), 9th (D#)

A
B♭/A#
B
C
C#/D♭
D
E♭/D#
E
F
F#/G♭
G
A♭/G#
Other Chords

C♯6sus4

6th Suspended 4th

(Left Hand)

C♯D♭   D♯E♭   F♯G♭   G♯A♭   A♯B♭

C   D   E   F   G   A   B

5 = little finger   4 = ring finger   3 = middle finger   2 = index finger   1 = thumb

Chord Spelling

1st (C♯), 4th (F♯), 5th (G♯), 6th (A♯)

C♯6sus4

6th Suspended 4th

(**Right** Hand)

A

B♭/A♯

B

C

C♯/D♭

D

E♭/D♯

E

F

F♯/G♭

G

A♭/G♯

Other Chords

1 = thumb   2 = index finger   3 = middle finger   4 = ring finger   5 = little finger

Chord Spelling

1st (C♯), 4th (F♯), 5th (G♯), 6th (A♯)

C#maj7+5

Major 7th Augmented 5th

(**Left** Hand)

5 = little finger   4 = ring finger   3 = middle finger   2 = index finger   1 = thumb

Chord Spelling

1st (C#), 3rd (E#), #5th (Gx), 7th (B#)

C#maj7+5

Major 7th Augmented 5th

(**Right** Hand)

F#G♭ G#A♭ A#B♭   C#D♭ D#E♭

F G A B C D E

1 = thumb   2 = index finger   3 = middle finger   4 = ring finger   5 = little finger

Chord Spelling

1st (C#), 3rd (E#), #5th (Gx), 7th (B#)

A
B♭/A#
B
C
C#/D♭
D
E♭/D#
E
F
F#/G♭
G
A♭/G#
Other Chords

C#maj7sus4
Major 7th Suspended 4th
(**Left** Hand)

A
Bb/A#
B
C
C#/Db
D
Eb/D#
E
F
F#/Gb
G
Ab/G#
Other Chords

F#Gb   G#Ab   A#Bb   C#Db   D#Eb

Middle C

F   G   A   B   C   D   E

5 = little finger   4 = ring finger   3 = middle finger   2 = index finger   1 = thumb

Chord Spelling

1st (C#), 4th (F#), 5th (G#), 7th (B#)

C#maj7sus4
Major 7th Suspended 4th
(**Right** Hand)

A

B♭/A#

B

C

C#/D♭

D

E♭/D#

E

F

F#/G♭

G

A♭/G#

Other Chords

F#G♭   G#A♭   A#B♭   C#D♭   D#E♭

F   G   A   B   C   D   E

1 = thumb   2 = index finger   3 = middle finger   4 = ring finger   5 = little finger

Chord Spelling
1st (C#), 4th (F#), 5th (G#), 7th (B#)

C#m-maj7
Minor-Major 7th

(**Left** Hand)

F#G♭ G#A♭ A#B♭   C#D♭ D#E♭

Middle C

F G A B C D E

5 = little finger   4 = ring finger   3 = middle finger   2 = index finger   1 = thumb

Chord Spelling

1st (C#), ♭3rd (E), 5th (G#), 7th (B#)

C#m-maj7
Minor-Major 7th
(**Right** Hand)

F#G♭ G#A♭ A#B♭   C#D♭   D#E♭

F   G   A   B   C   D   E

1 = thumb   2 = index finger   3 = middle finger   4 = ring finger   5 = little finger

Chord Spelling

1st (C#), ♭3rd (E), 5th (G#), 7th (B#)

A

B♭/A#

B

C

C#/D♭

D

E♭/D#

E

F

F#/G♭

G

A♭/G#

Other Chords

C#maj9

Major 9th

(**Left** Hand)

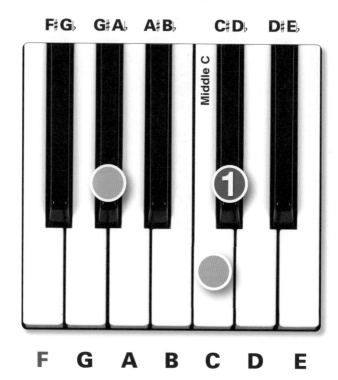

F#G♭ G#A♭ A#B♭   C#D♭   D#E♭

Middle C

F   G   A   B   C   D   E

5 = little finger   4 = ring finger   3 = middle finger   2 = index finger   1 = thumb

Chord Spelling

1st (C#), 3rd (E#), 5th (G#), 7th (B#), 9th (D#)

C#maj9

Major 9th

(**Right** Hand)

A

B♭/A♯

B

C

C♯/D♭

D

E♭/D♯

E

F

F♯/G♭

G

A♭/G♯

Other Chords

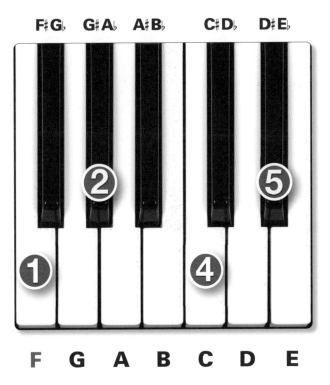

F♯G♭   G♯A♭   A♯B♭   C♯D♭   D♯E♭

F   G   A   B   C   D   E

1 = thumb   2 = index finger   3 = middle finger   4 = ring finger   5 = little finger

Chord Spelling

1st (C#), 3rd (E#), 5th (G#), 7th (B#), 9th (D#)

C#m9

Minor 9th

(**Left** Hand)

F#G♭ **G#A♭** **A#B♭** **C#D♭** **D#E♭**

Middle C

F G A B C D E

5 = little finger   4 = ring finger   3 = middle finger   2 = index finger   1 = thumb

Chord Spelling

1st (C#), ♭3rd (E), 5th (G#), ♭7th (B), 9th (D#)

C#m9

Minor 9th

(**Right** Hand)

F#G♭ G#A♭ A#B♭   C#D♭   D#E♭

F   G   A   B   C   D   E

1 = thumb 2 = index finger 3 = middle finger 4 = ring finger 5 = little finger

Chord Spelling

1st (C#), ♭3rd (E), 5th (G#), ♭7th (B), 9th (D#)

A

B♭/A#

B

C

C#/D♭

D

E♭/D#

E

F

F#/G♭

G

A♭/G#

Other
Chords

C#m-maj9
Minor-Major 9th

(**Left** Hand)

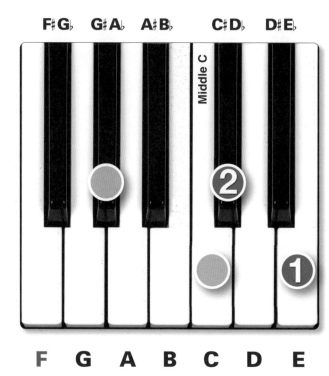

5 = little finger   4 = ring finger   3 = middle finger   2 = index finger   1 = thumb

Chord Spelling

1st (C#), b3rd (E), 5th (G#), 7th (B#), 9th (D#)

C#m-maj9

Minor-Major 9th

(**Right** Hand)

F#G♭   G#A♭   A#B♭   C#D♭   D#E♭

F   G   A   B   C   D   E

A
B♭/A#
B
C
C#/D♭
D
E♭/D#
E
F
F#/G♭
G
A♭/G#
Other Chords

1 = thumb   2 = index finger   3 = middle finger   4 = ring finger   5 = little finger

Chord Spelling

1st (C#), ♭3rd (E), 5th (G#), 7th (B#), 9th (D#)

C#maj11

Major 11th

(**Left** Hand)

G#A♭ A#B♭   C#D♭   D#E♭   F#G♭

Middle C

④

①

A   B   C   D   E   F   G

5 = little finger   4 = ring finger   3 = middle finger   2 = index finger   1 = thumb

Chord Spelling

1st (C#), 3rd (E#), 5th (G#), 7th (B#),
9th (D#), 11th (F#)

C#maj11

Major 11th

(**Right** Hand)

A

B♭/A#

B

C

C#/D♭

D

E♭/D#

E

F

F#/G♭

G

A♭/G#

Other Chords

G#A♭ A#B♭   C#D♭   D#E♭   F#G♭

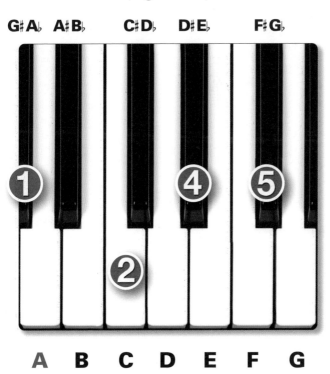

A   B   C   D   E   F   G

1 = thumb   2 = index finger   3 = middle finger   4 = ring finger   5 = little finger

Chord Spelling

1st (C#), 3rd (E#), 5th (G#), 7th (B#),
9th (D#), 11th (F#)

C#m11

Minor 11th

(**Left** Hand)

G#A♭   A#B♭   C#D♭   D#E♭   F#G♭

Middle C

④   ①

A   **B**   **C**   **D**   **E**   **F**   **G**

5 = little finger 4 = ring finger 3 = middle finger 2 = index finger 1 = thumb

Chord Spelling

1st (C#), ♭3rd (E), 5th (G#), ♭7th (B),
9th (D#), 11th (F#)

C#m11

Minor 11th

(**Right** Hand)

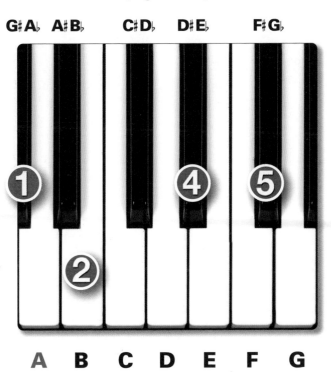

G#A♭ A#B♭ C#D♭ D#E♭ F#G♭

A B C D E F G

1 = thumb 2 = index finger 3 = middle finger 4 = ring finger 5 = little finger

A

B♭/A#

B

C

C#/D♭

D

E♭/D#

E

F

F#/G♭

G

A♭/G#

Other Chords

Chord Spelling

1st (C#), ♭3rd (E), 5th (G#), ♭7th (B),
9th (D#), 11th (F#)

C#/D♭ 11

Dominant 11th

(**Left** Hand)

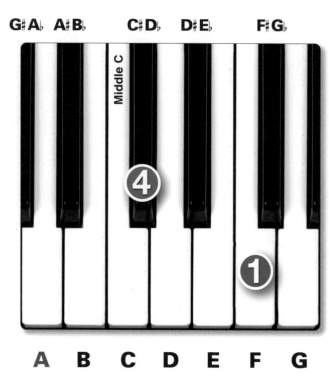

G#A♭ A#B♭   C#D♭   D#E♭   F#G♭

Middle C

④

①

A   B   C   D   E   F   G

5 = little finger   4 = ring finger   3 = middle finger   2 = index finger   1 = thumb

Chord Spelling

1st (C#), 3rd (E#), 5th (G#), ♭7th (B),
9th (D#), 11th (F#)

A
B♭/A#
B
C
C#/D♭
D
E♭/D#
E
F
F#/G♭
G
A♭/G#
Other Chords

C#/Db 11

Dominant 11th

(**Right** Hand)

A

Bb/A#

B

C

C#/Db

D

Eb/D#

E

F

F#/Gb

G

Ab/G#

Other Chords

G#Ab **A#Bb**   **C#Db** **D#Eb**   **F#Gb**

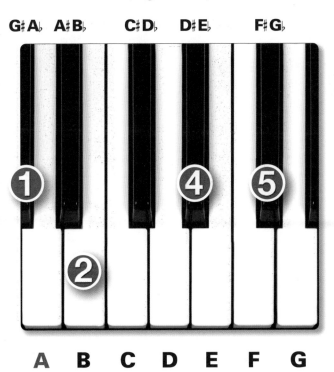

A   B   C   D   E   F   G

1 = thumb   2 = index finger   3 = middle finger   4 = ring finger   5 = little finger

Chord Spelling

1st (C#), 3rd (E#), 5th (G#), b7th (B),
9th (D#), 11th (F#)

C#maj13

Major 13th

(**Left** Hand)

5 = little finger 4 = ring finger 3 = middle finger 2 = index finger 1 = thumb

Chord Spelling

1st (C#), 3rd (E#), 5th (G#), 7th (B#),
9th (D#), 11th (F#), 13th (A#)

C♯maj13

Major 13th

(**Right** Hand)

1 = thumb 2 = index finger 3 = middle finger 4 = ring finger 5 = little finger

Chord Spelling

1st (C♯), 3rd (E♯), 5th (G♯), 7th (B♯),
9th (D♯), 11th (F♯), 13th (A♯)

A

B♭/A♯

B

C

C♯/D♭

D

E♭/D♯

E

F

F♯/G♭

G

A♭/G♯

Other Chords

C#m13

Minor 13th

(**Left** Hand)

C#D♭ D#E♭   F#G♭ G#A♭ A#B♭

C D E F G A B

5 = little finger 4 = ring finger 3 = middle finger 2 = index finger 1 = thumb

Chord Spelling

1st (C#), ♭3rd (E), 5th (G#), ♭7th (B),
9th (D#), 11th (F#), 13th (A#)

C#m13

Minor 13th

(**Right** Hand)

A

B♭/A#

B

C

C#/D♭

D

E♭/D#

E

F

F#/G♭

G

A♭/G#

Other Chords

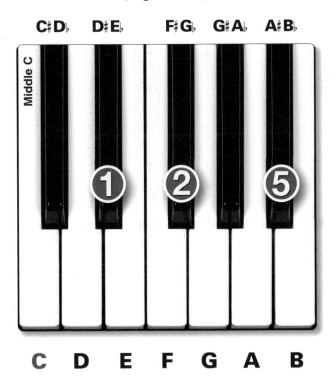

1 = thumb   2 = index finger   3 = middle finger   4 = ring finger   5 = little finger

Chord Spelling

1st (C#), ♭3rd (E), 5th (G#), ♭7th (B),
9th (D#), 11th (F#), 13th (A#)

C#13

Dominant 13th

(**Left** Hand)

C#D♭   D#E♭   F#G♭   G#A♭   A#B♭

C   D   E   F   G   A   B

5 = little finger   4 = ring finger   3 = middle finger   2 = index finger   1 = thumb

Chord Spelling

1st (C#), 3rd (E#), 5th (G#), ♭7th (B),
9th (D#), 11th (F#), 13th (A#)

A
B♭/A#
B
C
C#/D♭
D
E♭/D#
E
F
F#/G♭
G
A♭/G#
Other Chords

C#13

Dominant 13th

(**Right** Hand)

A

B♭/A#

B

C

C#/D♭

D

E♭/D#

E

F

F#/G♭

G

A♭/G#

Other
Chords

C#D♭   D#E♭   F#G♭   G#A♭   A#B♭

C   D   E   F   G   A   B

1 = thumb   2 = index finger   3 = middle finger   4 = ring finger   5 = little finger

Chord Spelling

1st (C#), 3rd (E#), 5th (G#), ♭7th (B),
9th (D#), 11th (F#), 13th (A#)

Dmaj6/9
Major 6th add 9th

(**Left** Hand)

F#G♭ G#A♭ A#B♭ C#D♭ D#E♭

Middle C

F G A B C D E

5 = little finger   4 = ring finger   3 = middle finger   2 = index finger   1 = thumb

Chord Spelling

1st (D), 3rd (F#), 5th (A), 6th (B), 9th (E)

A
B♭/A#
B
C
C#/D♭
D
E♭/D#
E
F
F#/G♭
G
A♭/G#
Other Chords

Dmaj6/9

Major 6th add 9th

(**Right** Hand)

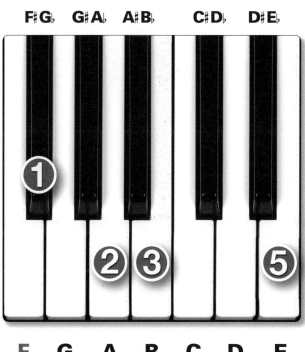

F#G♭ G#A♭ A#B♭   C#D♭   D#E♭

F G A B C D E

1 = thumb 2 = index finger 3 = middle finger 4 = ring finger 5 = little finger

Chord Spelling

1st (D), 3rd (F#), 5th (A), 6th (B), 9th (E)

Dm6/9

Minor 6th add 9th

(**Left** Hand)

F#G♭ G#A♭ A#B♭   C#D♭ D#E♭

Middle C

F G A B C D E

5 = little finger   4 = ring finger   3 = middle finger   2 = index finger   1 = thumb

Chord Spelling

1st (D), ♭3rd (F), 5th (A), 6th (B), 9th (E)

Dm6/9

Minor 6th add 9th

(**Right** Hand)

F#G♭ G#A♭ A#B♭   C#D♭   D#E♭

F G A B C D E

A
B♭/A#
B
C
C#/D♭
D
E♭/D#
E
F
F#/G♭
G
A♭/G#
Other Chords

1 = thumb   2 = index finger   3 = middle finger   4 = ring finger   5 = little finger

Chord Spelling

1st (D), ♭3rd (F), 5th (A), 6th (B), 9th (E)

D6sus4

6th Suspended 4th

(**Left** Hand)

C♯D♭ **D♯E♭**   **F♯G♭** **G♯A♭** **A♯B♭**

C D E F G A B

5 = little finger   4 = ring finger   3 = middle finger   2 = index finger   1 = thumb

A
B♭/A♯
B
C
C♯/D♭
D
E♭/D♯
E
F
F♯/G♭
G
A♭/G♯
Other Chords

Chord Spelling

1st (D), 4th (G), 5th (A), 6th (B)

D6sus4

6th Suspended 4th

(**Right** Hand)

A
B♭/A♯
B
C
C♯/D♭
D
E♭/D♯
E
F
F♯/G♭
G
A♭/G♯
Other Chords

C♯D♭ D♯E♭   F♯G♭ G♯A♭ A♯B♭

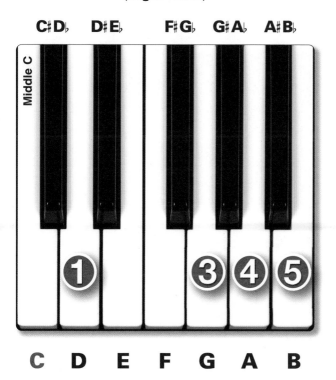

Middle C

C D E F G A B

1 = thumb   2 = index finger   3 = middle finger   4 = ring finger   5 = little finger

Chord Spelling

1st (D), 4th (G), 5th (A), 6th (B)

Dmaj7+5

Major 7th Augmented 5th

(**Left** Hand)

5 = little finger   4 = ring finger   3 = middle finger   2 = index finger   1 = thumb

Chord Spelling

1st (D), 3rd (F#), #5th (A#), 7th (C#)

Dmaj7+5

Major 7th Augmented 5th

(**Right** Hand)

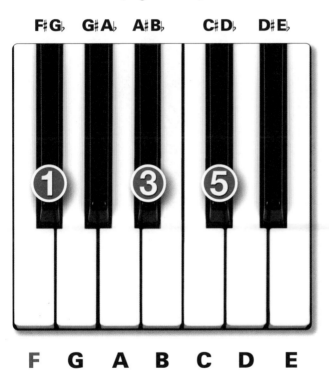

F#G♭   G#A♭   A#B♭   C#D♭   D#E♭

F   G   A   B   C   D   E

1 = thumb   2 = index finger   3 = middle finger   4 = ring finger   5 = little finger

Chord Spelling

1st (D), 3rd (F#), #5th (A#), 7th (C#)

A
B♭/A#
B
C
C#/D♭
D
E♭/D#
E
F
F#/G♭
G
A♭/G#
Other Chords

Dmaj7sus4
Major 7th Suspended 4th
(**Left** Hand)

5 = little finger   4 = ring finger   3 = middle finger   2 = index finger   1 = thumb

Chord Spelling

1st (D), 4th (G), 5th (A), 7th (C♯)

Dmaj7sus4

Major 7th Suspended 4th

(**Right** Hand)

F#G♭ G#A♭ A#B♭   C#D♭   D#E♭

F G A B C D E

1 = thumb 2 = index finger 3 = middle finger 4 = ring finger 5 = little finger

A
B♭/A#
B
C
C#/D♭
D
E♭/D#
E
F
F#/G♭
G
A♭/G#
Other Chords

Chord Spelling

1st (D), 4th (G), 5th (A), 7th (C#)

Dm-maj7
Minor-Major 7th
(**Left** Hand)

F#G♭ G#A♭ A#B♭   C#D♭   D#E♭

Middle C

F G A B C D E

5 = little finger   4 = ring finger   3 = middle finger   2 = index finger   1 = thumb

Chord Spelling

1st (D), ♭3rd (F), 5th (A), 7th (C#)

A
B♭/A#
B
C
C#/D♭
D
E♭/D#
E
F
F#/G♭
G
A♭/G#
Other Chords

Dm-maj7
Minor-Major 7th
(Right Hand)

F#G♭ G#A♭ A#B♭   C#D♭   D#E♭

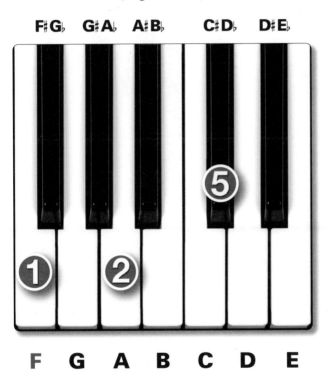

F   G   A   B   C   D   E

1 = thumb   2 = index finger   3 = middle finger   4 = ring finger   5 = little finger

Chord Spelling
1st (D), ♭3rd (F), 5th (A), 7th (C#)

A
B♭/A#
B
C
C#/D♭
D
E♭/D#
E
F
F#/G♭
G
A♭/G#
Other Chords

Dmaj9
Major 9th

(**Left** Hand)

5 = little finger   4 = ring finger   3 = middle finger   2 = index finger   1 = thumb

Chord Spelling

1st (D), 3rd (F#), 5th (A), 7th (C#), 9th (E)

Dmaj9
Major 9th
(**Right** Hand)

F♯G♭ G♯A♭ A♯B♭   C♯D♭   D♯E♭

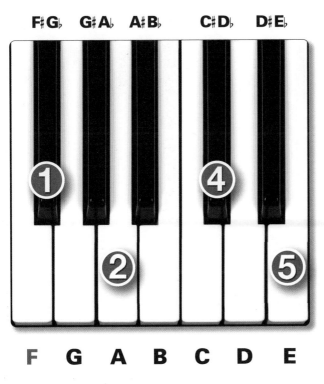

F G A B C D E

A   B♭/A♯   B   C   C♯/D♭   D   E♭/D♯   E   F   F♯/G♭   G   A♭/G♯   Other Chords

1 = thumb   2 = index finger   3 = middle finger   4 = ring finger   5 = little finger

Chord Spelling
1st (D), 3rd (F♯), 5th (A), 7th (C♯), 9th (E)

Dm9

Minor 9th

(**Left** Hand)

5 = little finger   4 = ring finger   3 = middle finger   2 = index finger   1 = thumb

Chord Spelling

1st (D), ♭3rd (F), 5th (A), ♭7th (C), 9th (E)

Dm9

Minor 9th

(**Right** Hand)

F#G♭   G#A♭   A#B♭   C#D♭   D#E♭

F   G   A   B   C   D   E

1 = thumb   2 = index finger   3 = middle finger   4 = ring finger   5 = little finger

Chord Spelling

1st (D), ♭3rd (F), 5th (A), ♭7th (C), 9th (E)

A

B♭/A#

B

C

C#/D♭

D

E♭/D#

E

F

F#/G♭

G

A♭/G#

Other Chords

Dm-maj9
Minor-Major 9th
(**Left** Hand)

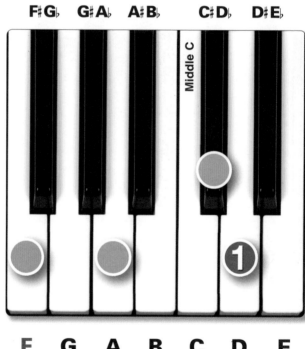

F#G♭ G#A♭ A#B♭   C#D♭   D#E♭

Middle C

F G A B C D E

5 = little finger 4 = ring finger 3 = middle finger 2 = index finger 1 = thumb

Chord Spelling

1st (D), ♭3rd (F), 5th (A), 7th (C#), 9th (E)

Dm-maj9
Minor-Major 9th
(**Right** Hand)

F♯G♭   G♯A♭   A♯B♭   C♯D♭   D♯E♭

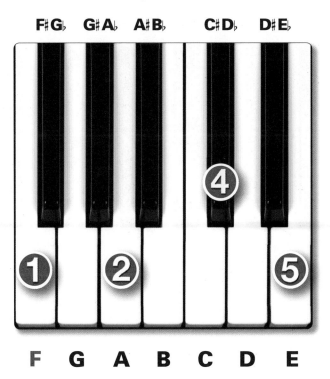

F   G   A   B   C   D   E

1 = thumb   2 = index finger   3 = middle finger   4 = ring finger   5 = little finger

A

B♭/A♯

B

C

C♯/D♭

D

E♭/D♯

E

F

F♯/G♭

G

A♭/G♯

Other Chords

Chord Spelling

1st (D), ♭3rd (F), 5th (A), 7th (C♯), 9th (E)

Dmaj11
Major 11th

(**Left** Hand)

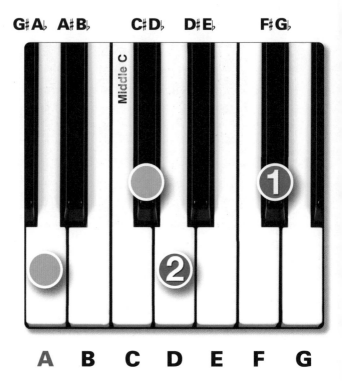

G#A♭ A#B♭   C#D♭   D#E♭   F#G♭

Middle C

A   B   C   D   E   F   G

5 = little finger   4 = ring finger   3 = middle finger   2 = index finger   1 = thumb

Chord Spelling

1st (D), 3rd (F#), 5th (A), 7th (C#),
9th (E), 11th (G)

Dmaj11

Major 11th

(**Right** Hand)

G#A♭ A#B♭   C#D♭   D#E♭   F#G♭

A B C D E F G

1 = thumb   2 = index finger   3 = middle finger   4 = ring finger   5 = little finger

Chord Spelling

1st (D), 3rd (F#), 5th (A), 7th (C#),
9th (E), 11th (G)

A

B♭/A#

B

C

C#/D♭

D

E♭/D#

E

F

F#/G♭

G

A♭/G#

Other
Chords

A

B♭/A♯

B

C

C♯/D♭

D

E♭/D♯

E

F

F♯/G♭

G

A♭/G♯

Other
Chords

Dm11

Minor 11th

(**Left** Hand)

G♯A♭ **A♯B♭**   **C♯D♭** **D♯E♭**   **F♯G♭**

Middle C

A   **B**   **C**   **D**   **E**   **F**   **G**

5 = little finger   4 = ring finger   3 = middle finger   2 = index finger   1 = thumb

Chord Spelling

1st (D), ♭3rd (F), 5th (A), ♭7th (C),
9th (E), 11th (G)

Dm11

Minor 11th

(**Right** Hand)

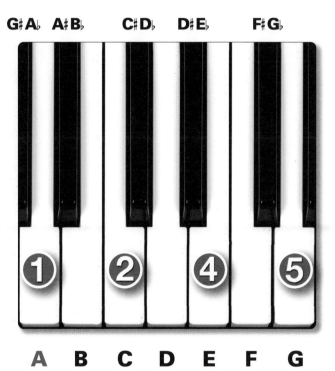

G#A♭ A#B♭   C#D♭   D#E♭   F#G♭

①   ②   ④   ⑤

A   B   C   D   E   F   G

1 = thumb   2 = index finger   3 = middle finger   4 = ring finger   5 = little finger

Chord Spelling

1st (D), ♭3rd (F), 5th (A), ♭7th (C),
9th (E), 11th (G)

D11

Dominant 11th

(**Left** Hand)

G#A♭ A#B♭   C#D♭   D#E♭   F#G♭

Middle C

① ② ⬤ ⬤

A B C D E F G

5 = little finger   4 = ring finger   3 = middle finger   2 = index finger   1 = thumb

A
B♭/A#
B
C
C#/D♭
D
E♭/D#
E
F
F#/G♭
G
A♭/G#
Other
Chords

Chord Spelling

1st (D), 3rd (F#), 5th (A), ♭7th (C),
9th (E), 11th (G)

D11

Dominant 11th

(**Right** Hand)

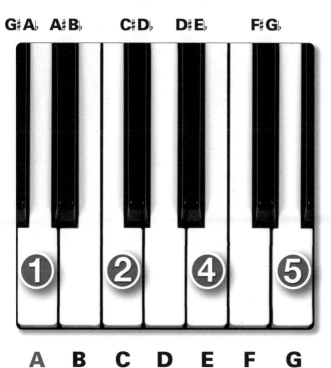

G#A♭ A#B♭   C#D♭   D#E♭   F#G♭

A   B   C   D   E   F   G

1 = thumb   2 = index finger   3 = middle finger   4 = ring finger   5 = little finger

A
B♭/A#
B
C
C#/D♭
D
E♭/D#
E
F
F#/G♭
G
A♭/G#
Other Chords

Chord Spelling

1st (D), 3rd (F#), 5th (A), ♭7th (C),
9th (E), 11th (G)

Dmaj13
Major 13th
(**Left** Hand)

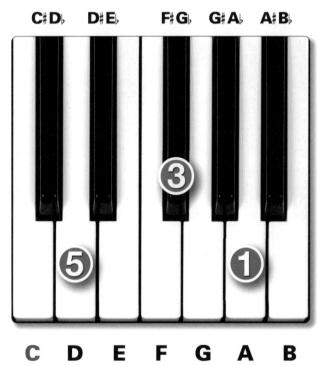

5 = little finger   4 = ring finger   3 = middle finger   2 = index finger   1 = thumb

Chord Spelling

1st (D), 3rd (F♯), 5th (A), 7th (C♯),
9th (E), 11th (G), 13th (B)

Dmaj13
Major 13th
(**Right** Hand)

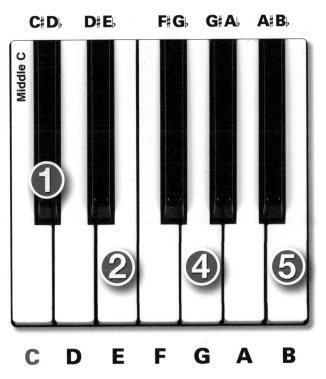

C#D♭   D#E♭   F#G♭   G#A♭   A#B♭

Middle C

① ② ④ ⑤

C D E F G A B

A
B♭/A#
B
C
C#/D♭
D
E♭/D#
E
F
F#/G♭
G
A♭/G#
Other Chords

1 = thumb   2 = index finger   3 = middle finger   4 = ring finger   5 = little finger

Chord Spelling

1st (D), 3rd (F#), 5th (A), 7th (C#),
9th (E), 11th (G), 13th (B)

Dm13
Minor 13th
(**Left** Hand)

C#D♭   D#E♭   F#G♭   G#A♭   A#B♭

C   D   E   F   G   A   B

5 = little finger   4 = ring finger   3 = middle finger   2 = index finger   1 = thumb

Chord Spelling

1st (D), ♭3rd (F), 5th (A), ♭7th (C),
9th (E), 11th (G), 13th (B)

Dm13

Minor 13th

(**Right** Hand)

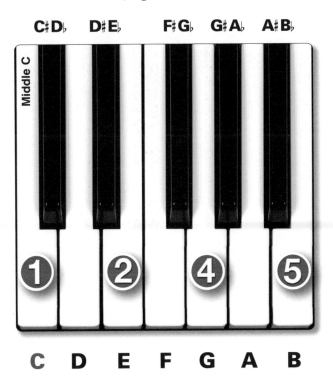

A

B♭/A♯

B

C

C♯/D♭

D

E♭/D♯

E

F

F♯/G♭

G

A♭/G♯

Other Chords

1 = thumb   2 = index finger   3 = middle finger   4 = ring finger   5 = little finger

Chord Spelling

1st (D), ♭3rd (F), 5th (A), ♭7th (C),
9th (E), 11th (G), 13th (B)

D13

Dominant 13th

(**Left** Hand)

5 = little finger   4 = ring finger   3 = middle finger   2 = index finger   1 = thumb

Chord Spelling

1st (D), 3rd (F♯), 5th (A), ♭7th (C),
9th (E), 11th (G), 13th (B)

D13

Dominant 13th

(**Right** Hand)

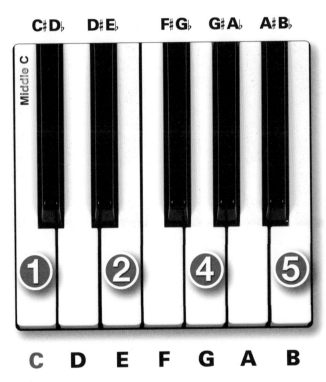

A

B♭/A♯

B

C

C♯/D♭

D

E♭/D♯

E

F

F♯/G♭

G

A♭/G♯

Other Chords

1 = thumb   2 = index finger   3 = middle finger   4 = ring finger   5 = little finger

Chord Spelling

1st (D), 3rd (F♯), 5th (A), ♭7th (C),
9th (E), 11th (G), 13th (B)

E♭maj6/9

Major 6th add 9th

(**Left** Hand)

5 = little finger   4 = ring finger   3 = middle finger   2 = index finger   1 = thumb

Chord Spelling

1st (E♭), 3rd (G), 5th (B♭), 6th (C), 9th (F)

E♭maj6/9
Major 6th add 9th

(**Right** Hand)

G♯A♭ **A♯B♭** **C♯D♭** **D♯E♭** **F♯G♭**

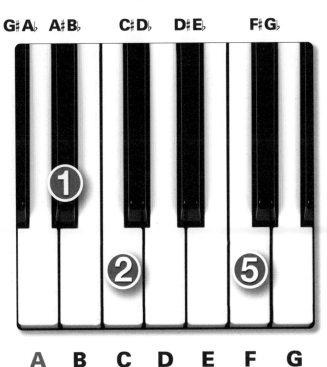

A B C D E F G

1 = thumb 2 = index finger 3 = middle finger 4 = ring finger 5 = little finger

Chord Spelling

1st (E♭), 3rd (G), 5th (B♭), 6th (C), 9th (F)

A
B♭/A♯
B
C
C♯/D♭
D
E♭/D♯
E
F
F♯/G♭
G
A♭/G♯
Other Chords

E♭m6/9

Minor 6th add 9th

(**Left** Hand)

G#A♭ A#B♭   C#D♭   D#E♭   F#G♭

Middle C

A B C D E F G

5 = little finger 4 = ring finger 3 = middle finger 2 = index finger 1 = thumb

Chord Spelling

1st (E♭), ♭3rd (G♭), 5th (B♭), 6th (C), 9th (F)

A
B♭/A#
B
C
C#/D♭
D
E♭/D#
E
F
F#/G♭
G
A♭/G#
Other Chords

E♭m6/9

Minor 6th add 9th

(**Right** Hand)

G#A♭ A#B♭   C#D♭ D#E♭   F#G♭

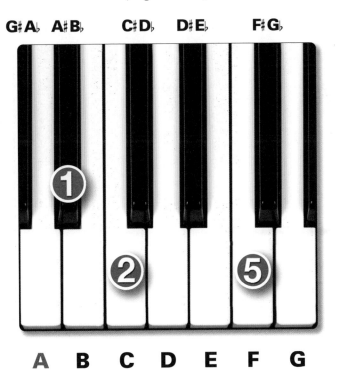

A   B   C   D   E   F   G

1 = thumb   2 = index finger   3 = middle finger   4 = ring finger   5 = little finger

Chord Spelling

1st (E♭), ♭3rd (G♭), 5th (B♭), 6th (C), 9th (F)

A

B♭/A#

B

C

C#/D♭

D

E♭/D#

E

F

F#/G♭

G

A♭/G#

Other Chords

E♭6sus4

6th Suspended 4th

(**Left** Hand)

F#G♭   G#A♭   A#B♭   C#D♭   D#E♭

Middle C

F   G   A   B   C   D   E

5 = little finger   4 = ring finger   3 = middle finger   2 = index finger   1 = thumb

Chord Spelling

1st (E♭), 4th (A♭), 5th (B♭), 6th (C)

A

B♭/A#

B

C

C#/D♭

D

E♭/D#

E

F

F#/G♭

G

A♭/G#

Other Chords

E♭6sus4

6th Suspended 4th

(**Right** Hand)

F♯G♭ **G♯A♭** **A♯B♭**   **C♯D♭**   **D♯E♭**

F   G   A   B   C   D   E

1 = thumb   2 = index finger   3 = middle finger   4 = ring finger   5 = little finger

Chord Spelling

1st (E♭), 4th (A♭), 5th (B♭), 6th (C)

A

B♭/A♯

B

C

C♯/D♭

D

E♭/D♯

E

F

F♯/G♭

G

A♭/G♯

Other Chords

E♭maj7+5

Major 7th Augmented 5th

(Left Hand)

5 = little finger   4 = ring finger   3 = middle finger   2 = index finger   1 = thumb

Chord Spelling

1st (E♭), 3rd (G), #5th (B), 7th (D)

E♭maj7+5

Major 7th Augmented 5th

(**Right** Hand)

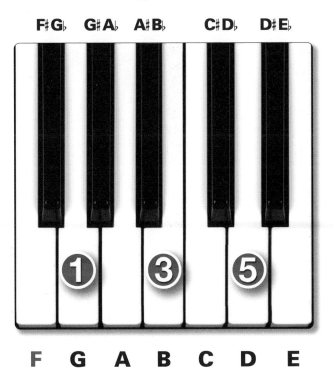

F#G♭ G#A♭ A#B♭   C#D♭ D#E♭

①   **③**   **⑤**

F G A B C D E

1 = thumb   2 = index finger   3 = middle finger   4 = ring finger   5 = little finger

Chord Spelling

1st (E♭), 3rd (G), #5th (B), 7th (D)

A

B♭/A#

B

C

C#/D♭

D

E♭/D#

E

F

F#/G♭

G

A♭/G#

Other
Chords

E♭maj7sus4

Major 7th Suspended 4th

(**Left** Hand)

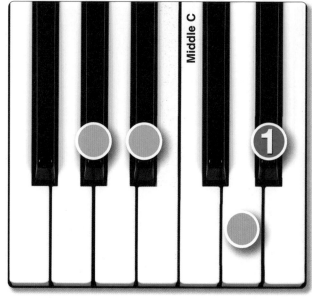

5 = little finger   4 = ring finger   3 = middle finger   2 = index finger   1 = thumb

Chord Spelling

1st (E♭), 4th (A♭), 5th (B♭), 7th (D)

E♭maj7sus4

Major 7th Suspended 4th

(**Right** Hand)

1 = thumb   2 = index finger   3 = middle finger   4 = ring finger   5 = little finger

Chord Spelling

1st (E♭), 4th (A♭), 5th (B♭), 7th (D)

B♭/A#
B
C
C#/D♭
D
E♭/D#
E
F
F#/G♭
G
A♭/G#
Other Chords

E♭m-maj7
Minor-Major 7th
(**Left** Hand)

F♯G♭   G♯A♭   A♯B♭   C♯D♭   D♯E♭

Middle C

F G A B C D E

5 = little finger   4 = ring finger   3 = middle finger   2 = index finger   1 = thumb

Chord Spelling
1st (E♭), ♭3rd (G♭), 5th (B♭), 7th (D)

A

B♭/A♯

B

C

C♯/D♭

D

E♭/D♯

E

F

F♯/G♭

G

A♭/G♯

Other Chords

E♭m-maj7

Minor-Major 7th

(**Right** Hand)

F♯G♭ G♯A♭ A♯B♭   C♯D♭ D♯E♭

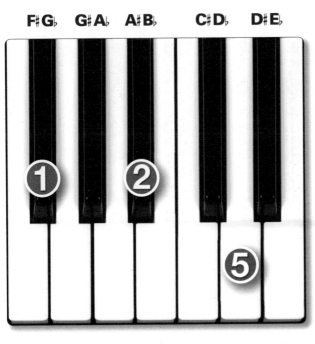

F   G   A   B   C   D   E

1 = thumb   2 = index finger   3 = middle finger   4 = ring finger   5 = little finger

Chord Spelling

1st (E♭), ♭3rd (G♭), 5th (B♭), 7th (D)

A
B♭/A♯
B
C
C♯/D♭
D
E♭/D♯
E
F
F♯/G♭
G
A♭/G♯
Other Chords

E♭maj9

Major 9th

(**Left** Hand)

G#A♭ A#B♭   C#D♭   D#E♭   F#G♭

Middle C

③   ①

A   B   C   D   E   F   G

5 = little finger   4 = ring finger   3 = middle finger   2 = index finger   1 = thumb

Chord Spelling

1st (E♭), 3rd (G), 5th (B♭), 7th (D), 9th (F)

A

B♭/A#

B

C

C#/D♭

D

E♭/D#

E

F

F#/G♭

G

A♭/G#

Other
Chords

E♭maj9

Major 9th

(**Right** Hand)

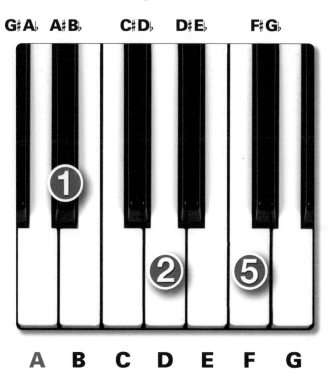

G♯A♭ A♯B♭   C♯D♭ D♯E♭   F♯G♭

A   B   C   D   E   F   G

1 = thumb   2 = index finger   3 = middle finger   4 = ring finger   5 = little finger

Chord Spelling

1st (E♭), 3rd (G), 5th (B♭), 7th (D), 9th (F)

A

B♭/A♯

B

C

C♯/D♭

D

E♭/D♯

E

F

F♯/G♭

G

A♭/G♯

Other
Chords

E♭m9

Minor 9th

(**Left** Hand)

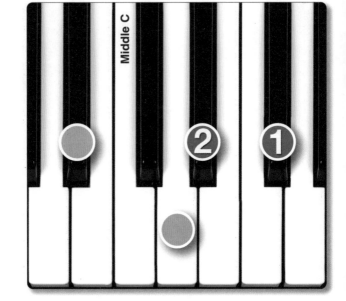

5 = little finger   4 = ring finger   3 = middle finger   2 = index finger   1 = thumb

Chord Spelling

1st (E♭), ♭3rd (G♭), 5th (B♭), ♭7th (D♭), 9th (F)

E♭m9

Minor 9th

(**Right** Hand)

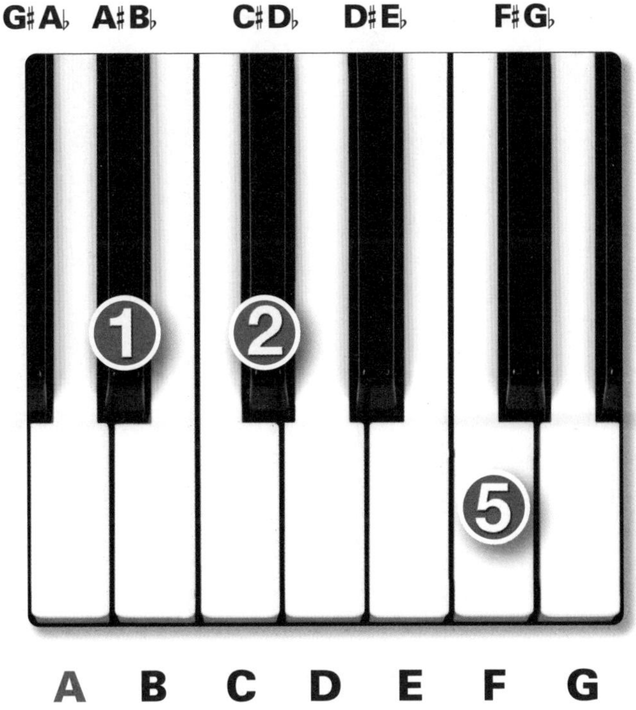
G♯A♭ A♯B♭ C♯D♭ D♯E♭ F♯G♭
1
2
5
A B C D E F G

1 = thumb 2 = index finger 3 = middle finger 4 = ring finger 5 = little finger

Chord Spelling

1st (E♭), ♭3rd (G♭), 5th (B♭), ♭7th (D♭), 9th (F)

A
B♭/A♯
B
C
C♯/D♭
D
E♭/D♯
E
F
F♯/G♭
G
A♭/G♯
Other Chords

E♭m-maj9

Minor-Major 9th

(**Left** Hand)

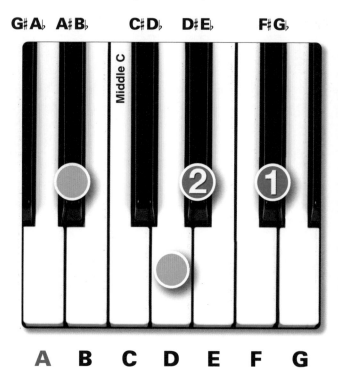

5 = little finger   4 = ring finger   3 = middle finger   2 = index finger   1 = thumb

Chord Spelling

1st (E♭), ♭3rd (G♭), 5th (B♭), 7th (D), 9th (F)

E♭m-maj9

Minor-Major 9th

(**Right** Hand)

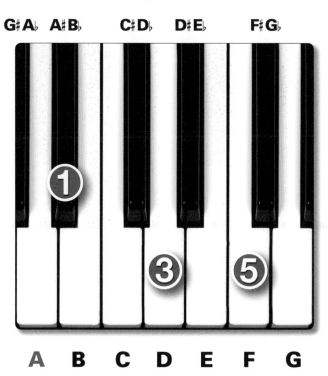

G#A♭ A#B♭   C#D♭   D#E♭   F#G♭

A   B   C   D   E   F   G

1 = thumb   2 = index finger   3 = middle finger   4 = ring finger   5 = little finger

A
B♭/A#
B
C
C#/D♭
D
E♭/D#
E
F
F#/G♭
G
A♭/G#
Other Chords

Chord Spelling

1st (E♭), ♭3rd (G♭), 5th (B♭), 7th (D), 9th (F)

E♭maj11
Major 11th
(**Left** Hand)

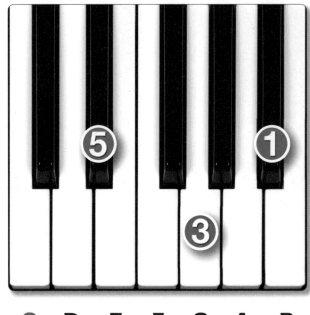

C♯D♭ D♯E♭ F♯G♭ G♯A♭ A♯B♭

C D E F G A B

5 = little finger   4 = ring finger   3 = middle finger   2 = index finger   1 = thumb

A
B♭/A♯
B
C
C♯/D♭
D
E♭/D♯
E
F
F♯/G♭
G
A♭/G♯
Other Chords

Chord Spelling

1st (E♭), 3rd (G), 5th (B♭), 7th (D),
9th (F), 11th (A♭)

E♭maj11

Major 11th

(Right Hand)

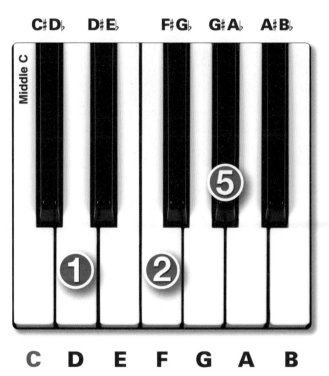

C♯D♭   D♯E♭   F♯G♭   G♯A♭   A♯B♭

Middle C

C   D   E   F   G   A   B

1 = thumb   2 = index finger   3 = middle finger   4 = ring finger   5 = little finger

A

B♭/A♯

B

C

C♯/D♭

D

E♭/D♯

E

F

F♯/G♭

G

A♭/G♯

Other Chords

Chord Spelling

1st (E♭), 3rd (G), 5th (B♭), 7th (D),
9th (F), 11th (A♭)

A
B♭/A♯
B
C
C♯/D♭
D
E♭/D♯
E
F
F♯/G♭
G
A♭/G♯
Other
Chords

E♭m11
Minor 11th

(**Left** Hand)

C♯D♭ D♯E♭ F♯G♭ G♯A♭ A♯B♭

⑤ ③ ①

C   D   E   F   G   A   B

5 = little finger   4 = ring finger   3 = middle finger   2 = index finger   1 = thumb

Chord Spelling

1st (E♭), ♭3rd (G♭), 5th (B♭), ♭7th (D♭),
9th (F), 11th (A♭)

E♭m11
Minor 11th
(**Right** Hand)

C#D♭ D#E♭   F#G♭ G#A♭ A#B♭

Middle C

C D E F G A B

1 = thumb   2 = index finger   3 = middle finger   4 = ring finger   5 = little finger

A

B♭/A#

B

C

C#/D♭

D

E♭/D#

E

F

F#/G♭

G

A♭/G#

Other
Chords

Chord Spelling

1st (E♭), ♭3rd (G♭), 5th (B♭), ♭7th (D♭),
9th (F), 11th (A♭)

E♭11

Dominant 11th

(**Left** Hand)

C♯D♭　D♯E♭　　F♯G♭　G♯A♭　A♯B♭

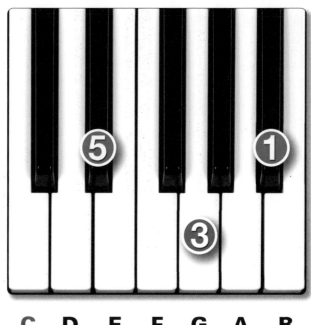

C　D　E　F　G　A　B

5 = little finger　4 = ring finger　3 = middle finger　2 = index finger　1 = thumb

Chord Spelling

1st (E♭), 3rd (G), 5th (B♭), ♭7th (D♭),
9th (F), 11th (A♭)

A
B♭/A♯
B
C
C♯/D♭
D
E♭/D♯
E
F
F♯/G♭
G
A♭/G♯
Other Chords

E♭11

Dominant 11th

(**Right** Hand)

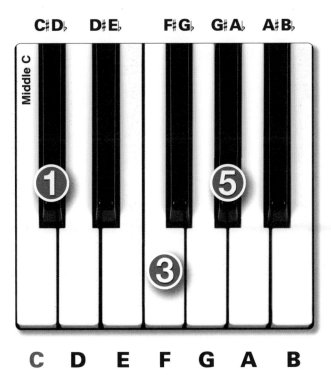

C♯D♭ D♯E♭ F♯G♭ G♯A♭ A♯B♭

C D E F G A B

1 = thumb   2 = index finger   3 = middle finger   4 = ring finger   5 = little finger

Chord Spelling

1st (E♭), 3rd (G), 5th (B♭), ♭7th (D♭),
9th (F), 11th (A♭)

A

B♭/A♯

B

C

C♯/D♭

D

E♭/D♯

E

F

F♯/G♭

G

A♭/G♯

Other
Chords

E♭maj13

Major 13th

(**Left** Hand)

D#E♭   F#G♭   G#A♭   A#B♭   C#D♭

Middle C

⑤   ②

④   ①

E   F   G   A   B   C   D

5 = little finger   4 = ring finger   3 = middle finger   2 = index finger   1 = thumb

Chord Spelling

1st (E♭), 3rd (G), 5th (B♭), 7th (D),
9th (F), 11th (A♭), 13th (C)

E♭maj13
Major 13th
(**Right** Hand)

A

B♭/A#

B

C

C#/D♭

D

E♭/D#

E

F

F#/G♭

G

A♭/G#

Other
Chords

D#E♭   F#G♭   G#A♭   A#B♭   C#D♭

E   F   G   A   B   C   D

1 = thumb   2 = index finger   3 = middle finger   4 = ring finger   5 = little finger

Chord Spelling

1st (E♭), 3rd (G), 5th (B♭), 7th (D),
9th (F), 11th (A♭), 13th (C)

E♭m13

Minor 13th

(**Left** Hand)

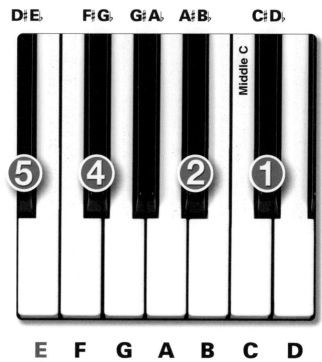

| D♯E♭ | F♯G♭ | G♯A♭ | A♯B♭ | C♯D♭ |

Middle C

⑤ ④ ② ①

E F G A B C D

5 = little finger   4 = ring finger   3 = middle finger   2 = index finger   1 = thumb

Chord Spelling

1st (E♭), ♭3rd (G♭), 5th (B♭), ♭7th (D♭),
9th (F), 11th (A♭), 13th (C)

E♭m13

Minor 13th

(**Right** Hand)

D♯E♭   F♯G♭ G♯A♭ A♯B♭   C♯D♭

E   F   G   A   B   C   D

1 = thumb   2 = index finger   3 = middle finger   4 = ring finger   5 = little finger

Chord Spelling

1st (E♭), ♭3rd (G♭), 5th (B♭), ♭7th (D♭),
9th (F), 11th (A♭), 13th (C)

A

B♭/A♯

B

C

C♯/D♭

D

E♭/D♯

E

F

F♯/G♭

G

A♭/G♯

Other
Chords

E♭13

Dominant 13th

(**Left** Hand)

D♯E♭   F♯G♭   G♯A♭   A♯B♭   C♯D♭

Middle C

⑤   ②   ①

④

E   F   G   A   B   C   D

5 = little finger   4 = ring finger   3 = middle finger   2 = index finger   1 = thumb

Chord Spelling

1st (E♭), 3rd (G), 5th (B♭), ♭7th (D♭),
9th (F), 11th (A♭), 13th (C)

A
B♭/A♯
B
C
C♯/D♭
D
E♭/D♯
E
F
F♯/G♭
G
A♭/G♯
Other Chords

E♭13

Dominant 13th

(**Right** Hand)

D#E♭   F#G♭   G#A♭   A#B♭   C#D♭

E   F   G   A   B   C   D

1 = thumb   2 = index finger   3 = middle finger   4 = ring finger   5 = little finger

Chord Spelling

1st (E♭), 3rd (G), 5th (B♭), ♭7th (D♭),
9th (F), 11th (A♭), 13th (C)

A
B♭/A#
B
C
C#/D♭
D
E♭/D#
E
F
F#/G♭
G
A♭/G#
Other Chords

Emaj6/9
Major 6th add 9th

(**Left** Hand)

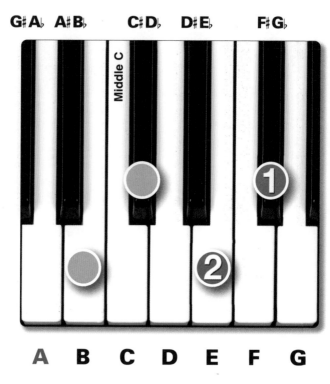

5 = little finger   4 = ring finger   3 = middle finger   2 = index finger   1 = thumb

Chord Spelling

1st (E), 3rd (G♯), 5th (B), 6th (C♯), 9th (F♯)

Emaj6/9

Major 6th add 9th

(**Right** Hand)

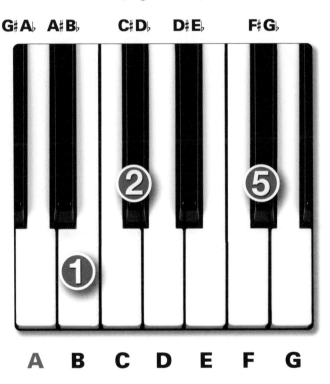

A   B   C   D   E   F   G

1 = thumb 2 = index finger 3 = middle finger 4 = ring finger 5 = little finger

Chord Spelling

1st (E), 3rd (G♯), 5th (B), 6th (C♯), 9th (F♯)

A

B♭/A♯

B

C

C♯/D♭

D

E♭/D♯

E

F

F♯/G♭

G

A♭/G♯

Other Chords

Em6/9

Minor 6th add 9th

(**Left** Hand)

G#A♭ **A#B♭** **C#D♭** **D#E♭** **F#G♭**

Middle C

A B C D E F G

5 = little finger   4 = ring finger   3 = middle finger   2 = index finger   1 = thumb

Chord Spelling

1st (E), ♭3rd (G), 5th (B), 6th (C#), 9th (F#)

A
B♭/A#
B
C
C#/D♭
D
E♭/D#
E
F
F#/G♭
G
A♭/G#
Other Chords

Em6/9
Minor 6th add 9th
(**Right** Hand)

G♯A♭ A♯B♭   C♯D♭   D♯E♭   F♯G♭

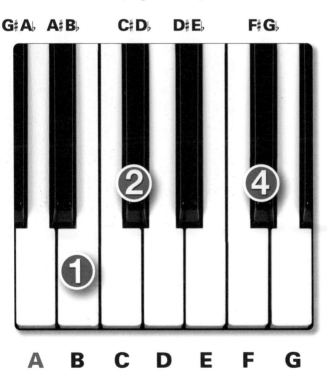

A   B   C   D   E   F   G

1 = thumb   2 = index finger   3 = middle finger   4 = ring finger   5 = little finger

Chord Spelling
1st (E), ♭3rd (G), 5th (B), 6th (C♯), 9th (F♯)

A
B♭/A♯
B
C
C♯/D♭
D
E♭/D♯
E
F
F♯/G♭
G
A♭/G♯
Other Chords

E6sus4

6th Suspended 4th

(**Left** Hand)

F#G♭ G#A♭ A#B♭ C#D♭ D#E♭

Middle C

F G A B C D E

5 = little finger   4 = ring finger   3 = middle finger   2 = index finger   1 = thumb

Chord Spelling

1st (E), 4th (A), 5th (B), 6th (C#)

E6sus4

6th Suspended 4th

(**Right** Hand)

F#G♭   G#A♭   A#B♭   C#D♭   D#E♭

F   G   A   B   C   D   E

1 = thumb   2 = index finger   3 = middle finger   4 = ring finger   5 = little finger

Chord Spelling

1st (E), 4th (A), 5th (B), 6th (C#)

A

B♭/A#

B

C

C#/D♭

D

E♭/D#

E

F

F#/G♭

G

A♭/G#

Other Chords

Emaj7+5

Major 7th Augmented 5th

(**Left** Hand)

5 = little finger 4 = ring finger 3 = middle finger 2 = index finger 1 = thumb

Chord Spelling

1st (E), 3rd (G#), #5th (B#), 7th (D#)

Emaj7+5

Major 7th Augmented 5th

(**Right** Hand)

F#G♭ G#A♭ A#B♭   C#D♭ D#E♭

F G A B C D E

A
B♭/A#
B
C
C#/D♭
D
E♭/D#
E
F
F#/G♭
G
A♭/G#

Other
Chords

1 = thumb   2 = index finger   3 = middle finger   4 = ring finger   5 = little finger

Chord Spelling

1st (E), 3rd (G#), #5th (B#), 7th (D#)

Emaj7sus4

Major 7th Suspended 4th

(**Left** Hand)

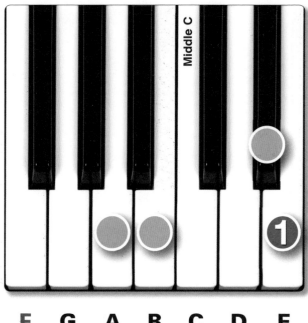

F#G♭   G#A♭   A#B♭   C#D♭   D#E♭

Middle C

F   G   A   B   C   D   E

5 = little finger   4 = ring finger   3 = middle finger   2 = index finger   1 = thumb

Chord Spelling

1st (E), 4th (A), 5th (B), 7th (D#)

A

B♭/A#

B

C

C#/D♭

D

E♭/D#

E

F

F#/G♭

G

A♭/G#

Other Chords

Emaj7sus4
Major 7th Suspended 4th
(Right Hand)

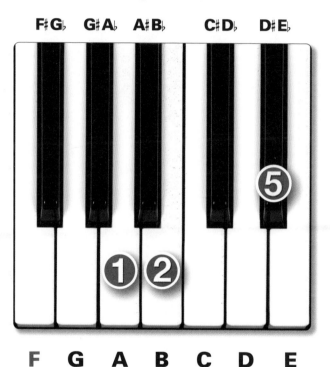

F#G♭   G#A♭   A#B♭   C#D♭   D#E♭

F   G   A   B   C   D   E

1 = thumb   2 = index finger   3 = middle finger   4 = ring finger   5 = little finger

Chord Spelling

1st (E), 4th (A), 5th (B), 7th (D#)

A
B♭/A#
B
C
C#/D♭
D
E♭/D#
E
F
F#/G♭
G
A♭/G#
Other Chords

Em-maj7

Minor-Major 7th

(**Left** Hand)

F#G♭   G#A♭   A#B♭   C#D♭   D#E♭

Middle C

F   G   A   B   C   D   E

5 = little finger   4 = ring finger   3 = middle finger   2 = index finger   1 = thumb

Chord Spelling

1st (E), ♭3rd (G), 5th (B), 7th (D♯)

Em-maj7
Minor-Major 7th

(**Right** Hand)

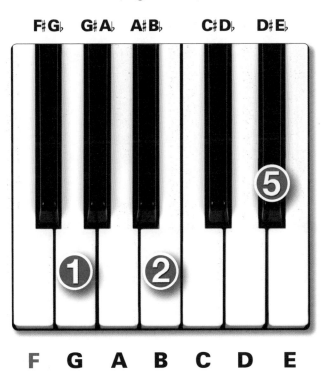

F#G♭ G#A♭ A#B♭   C#D♭   D#E♭

F G A B C D E

1 = thumb   2 = index finger   3 = middle finger   4 = ring finger   5 = little finger

A
B♭/A#
B
C
C#/D♭
D
E♭/D#
E
F
F#/G♭
G
A♭/G#
Other Chords

Chord Spelling

1st (E), ♭3rd (G), 5th (B), 7th (D#)

Emaj9
Major 9th
(**Left** Hand)

G#A♭   A#B♭   C#D♭   D#E♭   F#G♭

Middle C

A   B   C   D   E   F   G

5 = little finger   4 = ring finger   3 = middle finger   2 = index finger   1 = thumb

A
B♭/A#
B
C
C#/D♭
D
E♭/D#
E
F
F#/G♭
G
A♭/G#
Other Chords

Chord Spelling
1st (E), 3rd (G#), 5th (B), 7th (D#), 9th (F#)

Emaj9
Major 9th
(**Right** Hand)

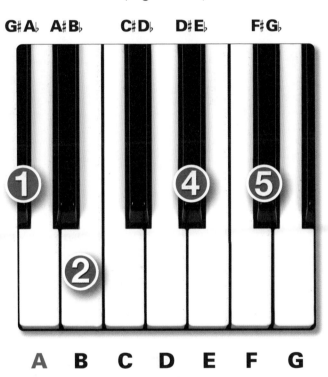

G♯A♭   A♯B♭   C♯D♭   D♯E♭   F♯G♭

A   B   C   D   E   F   G

1 = thumb   2 = index finger   3 = middle finger   4 = ring finger   5 = little finger

Chord Spelling

1st (E), 3rd (G♯), 5th (B), 7th (D♯), 9th (F♯)

A
B♭/A♯
B
C
C♯/D♭
D
E♭/D♯
E
F
F♯/G♭
G
A♭/G♯
Other Chords

Em9

Minor 9th

(**Left** Hand)

5 = little finger   4 = ring finger   3 = middle finger   2 = index finger   1 = thumb

Chord Spelling

1st (E), ♭3rd (G), 5th (B), ♭7th (D), 9th (F♯)

Em9

Minor 9th

(**Right** Hand)

G#A♭ A#B♭   C#D♭   D#E♭   F#G♭

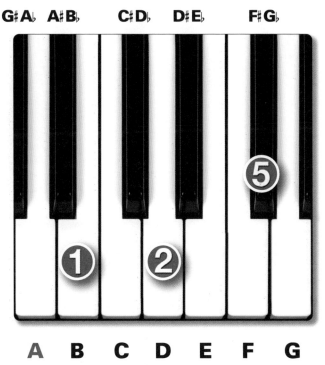

A   B   C   D   E   F   G

1 = thumb   2 = index finger   3 = middle finger   4 = ring finger   5 = little finger

Chord Spelling

1st (E), ♭3rd (G), 5th (B), ♭7th (D), 9th (F#)

A

B♭/A#

B

C

C#/D♭

D

E♭/D#

E

F

F#/G♭

G

A♭/G#

Other Chords

Em-maj9
Minor-Major 9th

(**Left** Hand)

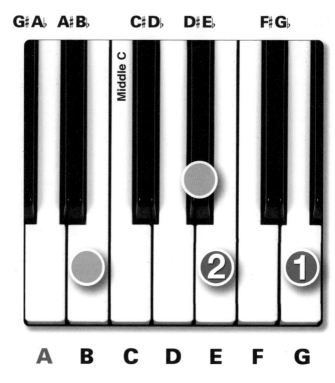

5 = little finger   4 = ring finger   3 = middle finger   2 = index finger   1 = thumb

Chord Spelling

1st (E), ♭3rd (G), 5th (B), 7th (D♯), 9th (F♯)

Em-maj9
Minor-Major 9th
(**Right** Hand)

G♯A♭ A♯B♭   C♯D♭   D♯E♭   F♯G♭

A B C D E F G

1 = thumb   2 = index finger   3 = middle finger   4 = ring finger   5 = little finger

Chord Spelling

1st (E), ♭3rd (G), 5th (B), 7th (D♯), 9th (F♯)

A

B♭/A♯

B

C

C♯/D♭

D

E♭/D♯

E

F

F♯/G♭

G

A♭/G♯

Other Chords

Emaj11

Major 11th

(**Left** Hand)

5 = little finger   4 = ring finger   3 = middle finger   2 = index finger   1 = thumb

Chord Spelling

1st (E), 3rd (G♯), 5th (B), 7th (D♯),
9th (F♯), 11th (A)

Emaj11
Major 11th
(**Right** Hand)

C#D♭   D#E♭   F#G♭   G#A♭   A#B♭

Middle C

C D E F G A B

1 = thumb   2 = index finger   3 = middle finger   4 = ring finger   5 = little finger

Chord Spelling

1st (E), 3rd (G#), 5th (B), 7th (D#),
9th (F#), 11th (A)

A
B♭/A#
B
C
C#/D♭
D
E♭/D#
E
F
F#/G♭
G
A♭/G#
Other Chords

Em11
Minor 11th

(**Left** Hand)

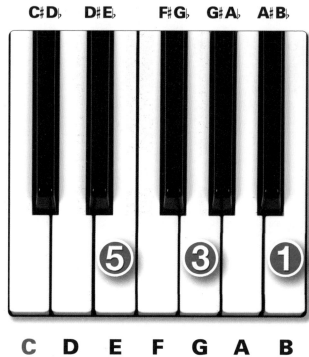

C#D♭   D#E♭   F#G♭   G#A♭   A#B♭

⑤   ③   ①

C   D   E   F   G   A   B

5 = little finger   4 = ring finger   3 = middle finger   2 = index finger   1 = thumb

Chord Spelling

1st (E), ♭3rd (G), 5th (B), ♭7th (D),
9th (F#), 11th (A)

Em11

Minor 11th

(**Right** Hand)

C♯D♭　D♯E♭　　F♯G♭　G♯A♭　A♯B♭

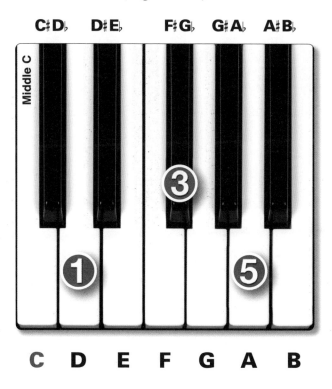

C　D　E　F　G　A　B

1 = thumb　2 = index finger　3 = middle finger　4 = ring finger　5 = little finger

Chord Spelling

1st (E), ♭3rd (G), 5th (B), ♭7th (D),
9th (F♯), 11th (A)

A
B♭/A♯
B
C
C♯/D♭
D
E♭/D♯
E
F
F♯/G♭
G
A♭/G♯
Other Chords

E11

Dominant 11th

(**Left** Hand)

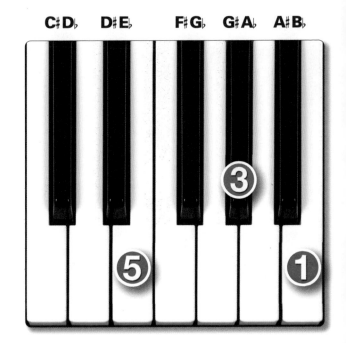

C#D♭ **D#E♭**   **F#G♭** **G#A♭** **A#B♭**

C   D   E   F   G   A   B

5 = little finger   4 = ring finger   3 = middle finger   2 = index finger   1 = thumb

Chord Spelling

1st (E), 3rd (G#), 5th (B), ♭7th (D),
9th (F#), 11th (A)

A
B♭/A#
B
C
C#/D♭
D
E♭/D#
E
F
F#/G♭
G
A♭/G#
Other Chords

E11

Dominant 11th

(**Right** Hand)

C♯D♭ D♯E♭   F♯G♭ G♯A♭ A♯B♭

Middle C

C D E F G A B

1 = thumb   2 = index finger   3 = middle finger   4 = ring finger   5 = little finger

Chord Spelling

1st (E), 3rd (G♯), 5th (B), ♭7th (D),
9th (F♯), 11th (A)

A

B♭/A♯

B

C

C♯/D♭

D

E♭/D♯

E

F

F♯/G♭

G

A♭/G♯

Other
Chords

Emaj13

Major 13th

(Left Hand)

| | D#E♭ | | F#G♭ | G#A♭ | A#B♭ | | C#D♭ | |

Middle C

⑤ ① ③

E F G A B C D

5 = little finger   4 = ring finger   3 = middle finger   2 = index finger   1 = thumb

Chord Spelling

1st (E), 3rd (G#), 5th (B), 7th (D#),
9th (F#), 11th (A), 13th (C#)

Emaj13

Major 13th

(**Right** Hand)

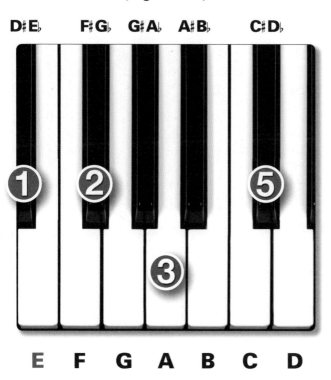

D#E♭   F#G♭ G#A♭ A#B♭   C#D♭

E   F   G   A   B   C   D

1 = thumb 2 = index finger 3 = middle finger 4 = ring finger 5 = little finger

A

B♭/A#

B

C

C#/D♭

D

E♭/D#

E

F

F#/G♭

G

A♭/G#

Other Chords

Chord Spelling

1st (E), 3rd (G#), 5th (B), 7th (D#),
9th (F#), 11th (A), 13th (C#)

Em13

Minor 13th

(**Left** Hand)

D#E♭   F#G♭   G#A♭   A#B♭   C#D♭

Middle C

⑤   ④   ②   ①

E   F   G   A   B   C   D

5 = little finger   4 = ring finger   3 = middle finger   2 = index finger   1 = thumb

Chord Spelling

1st (E), ♭3rd (G), 5th (B), ♭7th (D),
9th (F#), 11th (A), 13th (C#)

Em13

Minor 13th

(**Right** Hand)

D♯E♭ **F♯G♭** **G♯A♭** **A♯B♭** **C♯D♭**

E   F   G   A   B   C   D

1 = thumb   2 = index finger   3 = middle finger   4 = ring finger   5 = little finger

Chord Spelling

1st (E), ♭3rd (G), 5th (B), ♭7th (D),
9th (F♯), 11th (A), 13th (C♯)

A

B♭/A♯

B

C

C♯/D♭

D

E♭/D♯

E

F

F♯/G♭

G

A♭/G♯

Other
Chords

E13

Dominant 13th

(**Left** Hand)

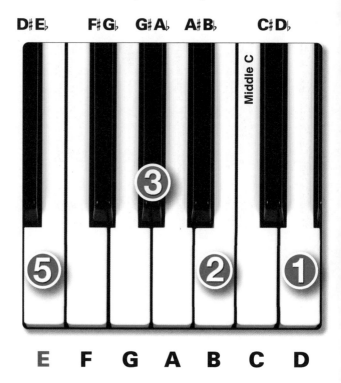

5 = little finger 4 = ring finger 3 = middle finger 2 = index finger 1 = thumb

Chord Spelling

1st (E), 3rd (G♯), 5th (B), ♭7th (D),
9th (F♯), 11th (A), 13th (C♯)

E13

Dominant 13th

(**Right** Hand)

1 = thumb   2 = index finger   3 = middle finger   4 = ring finger   5 = little finger

Chord Spelling

1st (E), 3rd (G♯), 5th (B), ♭7th (D),
9th (F♯), 11th (A), 13th (C♯)

A
B♭/A♯
B
C
C♯/D♭
D
E♭/D♯
E
F
F♯/G♭
G
A♭/G♯
Other Chords

Fmaj6/9
Major 6th add 9th

(**Left** Hand)

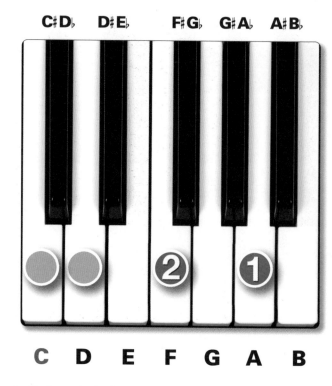

5 = little finger 4 = ring finger 3 = middle finger 2 = index finger 1 = thumb

Chord Spelling

1st (F), 3rd (A), 5th (C), 6th (D), 9th (G)

Fmaj6/9
Major 6th add 9th
(Right Hand)

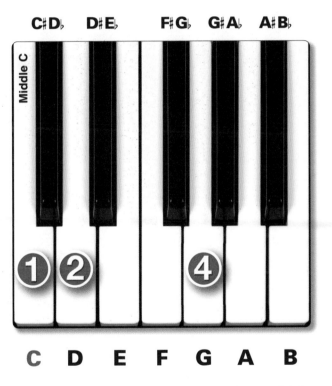

1 = thumb   2 = index finger   3 = middle finger   4 = ring finger   5 = little finger

Chord Spelling

1st (F), 3rd (A), 5th (C), 6th (D), 9th (G)

A
B♭/A♯
B
C
C♯/D♭
D
E♭/D♯
E
F
F♯/G♭
G
A♭/G♯
Other Chords

Fm6/9
Minor 6th add 9th
(**Left** Hand)

C#D♭   D#E♭   F#G♭   G#A♭   A#B♭

C   D   E   F   G   A   B

5 = little finger   4 = ring finger   3 = middle finger   2 = index finger   1 = thumb

Chord Spelling

1st (F), ♭3rd (A♭), 5th (C), 6th (D), 9th (G)

A
B♭/A#
B
C
C#/D♭
D
E♭/D#
E
F
F#/G♭
G
A♭/G#
Other Chords

Fm6/9

Minor 6th add 9th

(**Right** Hand)

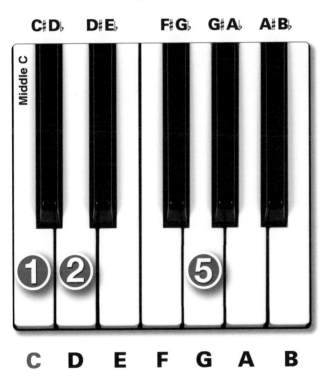

C#D♭ D#E♭ F#G♭ G#A♭ A#B♭

Middle C

① ② ⑤

C D E F G A B

A
B♭/A#
B
C
C#/D♭
D
E♭/D#
E
F
F#/G♭
G
A♭/G#
Other Chords

1 = thumb 2 = index finger 3 = middle finger 4 = ring finger 5 = little finger

Chord Spelling

1st (F), ♭3rd (A♭), 5th (C), 6th (D), 9th (G)

F6sus4

6th Suspended 4th

(**Left** Hand)

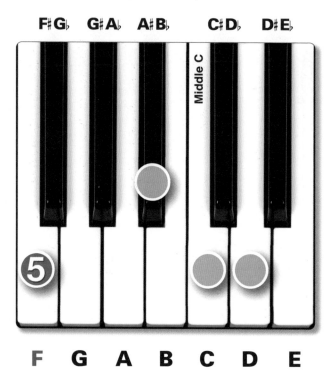

5 = little finger   4 = ring finger   3 = middle finger   2 = index finger   1 = thumb

Chord Spelling

1st (F), 4th (B♭), 5th (C), 6th (D)

F6sus4

6th Suspended 4th

(**Right** Hand)

F#G♭   G#A♭   A#B♭   C#D♭   D#E♭

F   G   A   B   C   D   E

1 = thumb   2 = index finger   3 = middle finger   4 = ring finger   5 = little finger

Chord Spelling

1st (F), 4th (B♭), 5th (C), 6th (D)

A

B♭/A#

B

C

C#/D♭

D

E♭/D#

E

F

F#/G♭

G

A♭/G#

Other Chords

A

B♭/A♯

B

C

C♯/D♭

D

E♭/D♯

E

F

F♯/G♭

G

A♭/G♯

Other
Chords

Fmaj7+5

Major 7th Augmented 5th

(**Left** Hand)

F♯G♭ G♯A♭ A♯B♭   C♯D♭ D♯E♭

Middle C

⑤

F   G   A   B   C   D   E

5 = little finger   4 = ring finger   3 = middle finger   2 = index finger   1 = thumb

Chord Spelling

1st (F), 3rd (A), ♯5th (C♯), 7th (E)

Fmaj7+5

Major 7th Augmented 5th

(Right Hand)

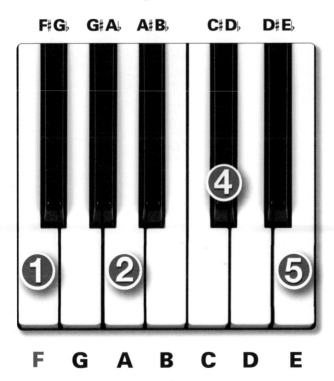

1 = thumb   2 = index finger   3 = middle finger   4 = ring finger   5 = little finger

Chord Spelling

1st (F), 3rd (A), ♯5th (C♯), 7th (E)

A
B♭/A♯
B
C
C♯/D♭
D
E♭/D♯
E
F
F♯/G♭
G
A♭/G♯
Other Chords

Fmaj7sus4
Major 7th Suspended 4th
(**Left** Hand)

5 = little finger   4 = ring finger   3 = middle finger   2 = index finger   1 = thumb

Chord Spelling
1st (F), 4th (B♭), 5th (C), 7th (E)

Fmaj7sus4

Major 7th Suspended 4th

(Right Hand)

F#G♭ G#A♭ A#B♭   C#D♭ D#E♭

F G A B C D E

1 = thumb   2 = index finger   3 = middle finger   4 = ring finger   5 = little finger

Chord Spelling

1st (F), 4th (B♭), 5th (C), 7th (E)

A
B♭/A#
B
C
C#/D♭
D
E♭/D#
E
F
F#/G♭
G
A♭/G#
Other Chords

Fm-maj7
Minor-Major 7th
(**Left** Hand)

5 = little finger   4 = ring finger   3 = middle finger   2 = index finger   1 = thumb

Chord Spelling

1st (F), ♭3rd (A♭), 5th (C), 7th (E)

Fm-maj7
Minor-Major 7th

(**Right** Hand)

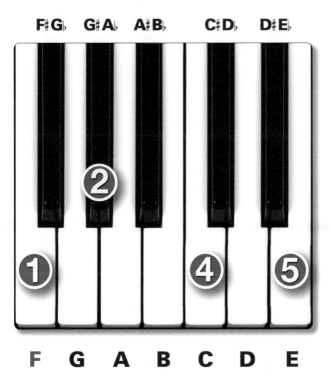

1 = thumb   2 = index finger   3 = middle finger   4 = ring finger   5 = little finger

Chord Spelling

1st (F), ♭3rd (A♭), 5th (C), 7th (E)

Fmaj9

Major 9th

(**Left** Hand)

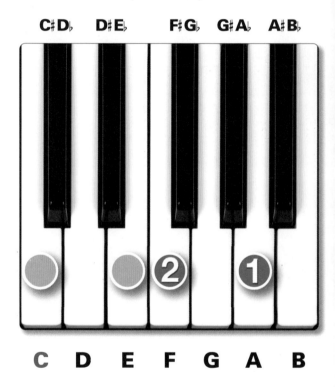

C#D♭   D#E♭   F#G♭   G#A♭   A#B♭

C   D   E   F   G   A   B

5 = little finger   4 = ring finger   3 = middle finger   2 = index finger   1 = thumb

Chord Spelling

1st (F), 3rd (A), 5th (C), 7th (E), 9th (G)

Fmaj9

Major 9th

(**Right** Hand)

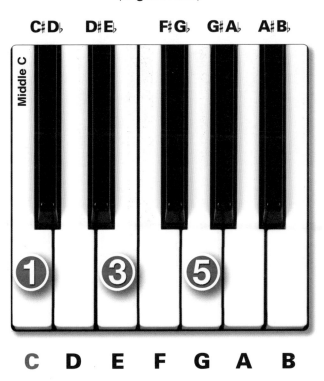

1 = thumb   2 = index finger   3 = middle finger   4 = ring finger   5 = little finger

Chord Spelling

1st (F), 3rd (A), 5th (C), 7th (E), 9th (G)

Fm9

Minor 9th

(Left Hand)

C#D♭ D#E♭   F#G♭ G#A♭ A#B♭

C   D   E   F   G   A   B

5 = little finger 4 = ring finger 3 = middle finger 2 = index finger 1 = thumb

Chord Spelling

1st (F), ♭3rd (A♭), 5th (C), ♭7th (E♭), 9th (G)

A

B♭/A#

B

C

C#/D♭

D

E♭/D#

E

F

F#/G♭

G

A♭/G#

Other
Chords

Fm9

Minor 9th

(Right Hand)

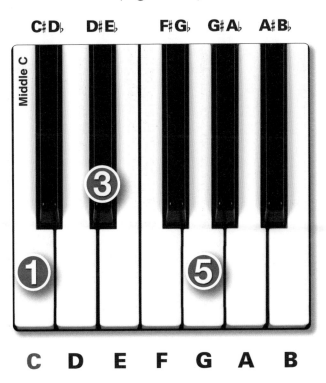

C#D♭   D#E♭   F#G♭   G#A♭   A#B♭

Middle C

C   D   E   F   G   A   B

A

B♭/A#

B

C

C#/D♭

D

E♭/D#

E

F

F#/G♭

G

A♭/G#

Other Chords

1 = thumb   2 = index finger   3 = middle finger   4 = ring finger   5 = little finger

Chord Spelling

1st (F), ♭3rd (A♭), 5th (C), ♭7th (E♭), 9th (G)

Fm-maj9
Minor-Major 9th
(**Left** Hand)

C#D♭ D#E♭ F#G♭ G#A♭ A#B♭

C D E F G A B

5 = little finger   4 = ring finger   3 = middle finger   2 = index finger   1 = thumb

Chord Spelling

1st (F), ♭3rd (A♭), 5th (C), 7th (E), 9th (G)

A

B♭/A#

B

C

C#/D♭

D

E♭/D#

E

F

F#/G♭

G

A♭/G#

Other
Chords

Fm-maj9
Minor-Major 9th

(**Right** Hand)

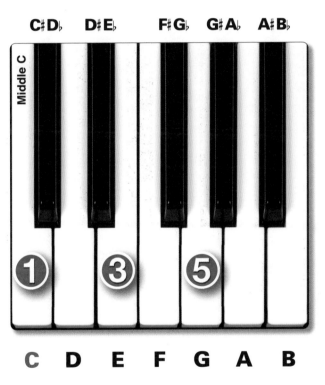

C#D♭ D#E♭   F#G♭ G#A♭ A#B♭

Middle C

① ③ ⑤

C D E F G A B

1 = thumb   2 = index finger   3 = middle finger   4 = ring finger   5 = little finger

Chord Spelling

1st (F), ♭3rd (A♭), 5th (C), 7th (E), 9th (G)

A

B♭/A#

B

C

C#/D♭

D

E♭/D#

E

F

F#/G♭

G

A♭/G#

Other Chords

Fmaj11

Major 11th

(**Left** Hand)

C#D♭   D#E♭   F#G♭   G#A♭   A#B♭

C   D   E   F   G   A   B

5 = little finger   4 = ring finger   3 = middle finger   2 = index finger   1 = thumb

Chord Spelling

1st (F), 3rd (A), 5th (C), 7th (E),
9th (G), 11th (B♭)

Fmaj11
Major 11th

(**Right** Hand)

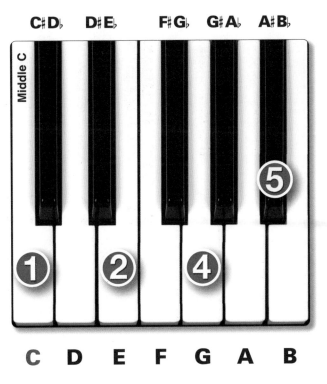

C#D♭   D#E♭   F#G♭   G#A♭   A#B♭

C D E F G A B

1 = thumb   2 = index finger   3 = middle finger   4 = ring finger   5 = little finger

A
B♭/A#
B
C
C#/D♭
D
E♭/D#
E
F
F#/G♭
G
A♭/G#
Other Chords

Chord Spelling

1st (F), 3rd (A), 5th (C), 7th (E),
9th (G), 11th (B♭)

Fm11
Minor 11th

(**Left** Hand)

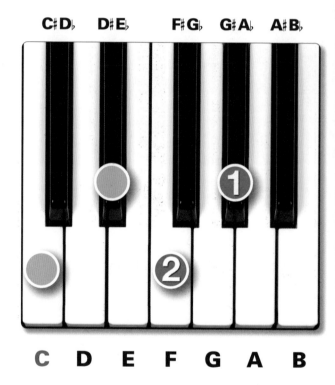

C#D♭   D#E♭   F#G♭   G#A♭   A#B♭

C   D   E   F   G   A   B

5 = little finger   4 = ring finger   3 = middle finger   2 = index finger   1 = thumb

Chord Spelling

1st (F), ♭3rd (A♭), 5th (C), ♭7th (E♭),
9th (G), 11th (B♭)

Fm11

Minor 11th

(**Right** Hand)

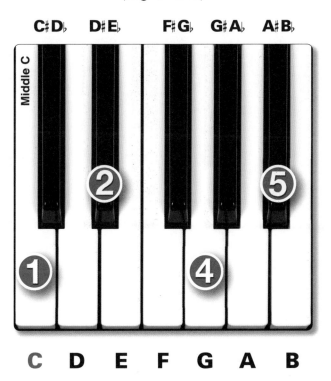

C♯D♭   D♯E♭   F♯G♭   G♯A♭   A♯B♭

Middle C

C   D   E   F   G   A   B

1 = thumb   2 = index finger   3 = middle finger   4 = ring finger   5 = little finger

Chord Spelling

1st (F), ♭3rd (A♭), 5th (C), ♭7th (E♭),
9th (G), 11th (B♭)

A

B♭/A♯

B

C

C♯/D♭

D

E♭/D♯

E

F

F♯/G♭

G

A♭/G♯

Other Chords

F11
Dominant 11th
(**Left** Hand)

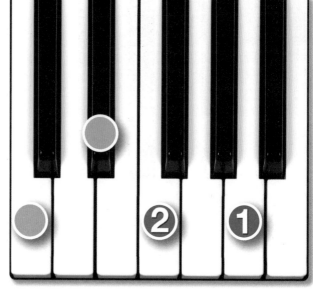

C♯D♭   D♯E♭   F♯G♭   G♯A♭   A♯B♭

C   D   E   F   G   A   B

5 = little finger   4 = ring finger   3 = middle finger   2 = index finger   1 = thumb

Chord Spelling

1st (F), 3rd (A), 5th (C), ♭7th (E♭),
9th (G), 11th (B♭)

F11

Dominant 11th

(**Right** Hand)

C#D♭   D#E♭   F#G♭   G#A♭   A#B♭

Middle C

C   D   E   F   G   A   B

1 = thumb   2 = index finger   3 = middle finger   4 = ring finger   5 = little finger

Chord Spelling

1st (F), 3rd (A), 5th (C), ♭7th (E♭),
9th (G), 11th (B♭)

A

B♭/A#

B

C

C#/D♭

D

E♭/D#

E

F

F#/G♭

G

A♭/G#

Other Chords

A
Bb/A#
B
C
C#/Db
D
Eb/D#
E
F
F#/Gb
G
Ab/G#
Other
Chords

Fmaj13
Major 13th

(**Left** Hand)

D#Eb   F#Gb   G#Ab   A#Bb   C#Db

Middle C

⑤   ③   ①

E   F   G   A   B   C   D

5 = little finger   4 = ring finger   3 = middle finger   2 = index finger   1 = thumb

Chord Spelling

1st (F), 3rd (A), 5th (C), 7th (E),
9th (G), 11th (Bb), 13th (D)

Fmaj13
Major 13th

(**Right** Hand)

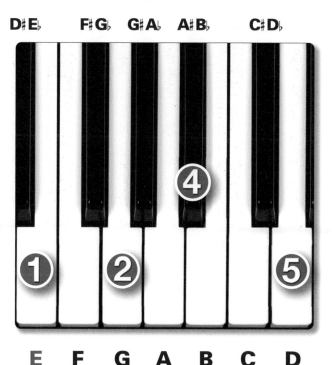

D#E♭   F#G♭ G#A♭ A#B♭   C#D♭

④

①   ②   ⑤

E   F   G   A   B   C   D

1 = thumb   2 = index finger   3 = middle finger   4 = ring finger   5 = little finger

Chord Spelling

1st (F), 3rd (A), 5th (C), 7th (E),
9th (G), 11th (B♭), 13th (D)

A

B♭/A#

B

C

C#/D♭

D

E♭/D#

E

F

F#/G♭

G

A♭/G#

Other
Chords

Fm13
Minor 13th

(**Left** Hand)

D#E♭   F#G♭   G#A♭   A#B♭   C#D♭

Middle C

③

⑤   ①

E   F   G   A   B   C   D

5 = little finger   4 = ring finger   3 = middle finger   2 = index finger   1 = thumb

Chord Spelling

1st (F), ♭3rd (A♭), 5th (C), ♭7th (E♭),
9th (G), 11th (B♭), 13th (D)

A
B♭/A#
B
C
C#/D♭
D
E♭/D#
E
F
F#/G♭
G
A♭/G#
Other Chords

Fm13
Minor 13th

(Right Hand)

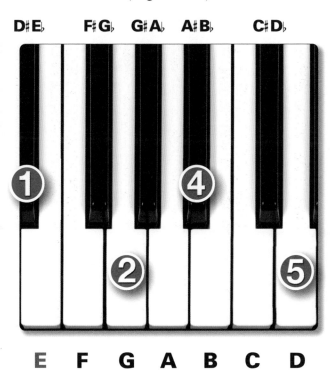

D#E♭   F#G♭ G#A♭ A#B♭   C#D♭

E F G A B C D

1 = thumb   2 = index finger   3 = middle finger   4 = ring finger   5 = little finger

Chord Spelling

1st (F), ♭3rd (A♭), 5th (C), ♭7th (E♭),
9th (G), 11th (B♭), 13th (D)

A
B♭/A#
B
C
C#/D♭
D
E♭/D#
E
F
F#/G♭
G
A♭/G#
Other Chords

F13

Dominant 13th

(**Left** Hand)

D#E♭　**F#G♭**　**G#A♭**　**A#B♭**　**C#D♭**

Middle C

⑤　③　①

E F G A B C D

5 = little finger   4 = ring finger   3 = middle finger   2 = index finger   1 = thumb

Chord Spelling

1st (F), 3rd (A), 5th (C), ♭7th (E♭),
9th (G), 11th (B♭), 13th (D)

A
B♭/A#
B
C
C#/D♭
D
E♭/D#
E
F
F#/G♭
G
A♭/G#
Other
Chords

F13

Dominant 13th

(**Right** Hand)

A

B♭/A♯

B

C

C♯/D♭

D

E♭/D♯

E

F

F♯/G♭

G

A♭/G♯

Other Chords

D♯E♭   F♯G♭ G♯A♭   A♯B♭   C♯D♭

E   F   G   A   B   C   D

1 = thumb   2 = index finger   3 = middle finger   4 = ring finger   5 = little finger

Chord Spelling

1st (F), 3rd (A), 5th (C), ♭7th (E♭),
9th (G), 11th (B♭), 13th (D)

F#maj6/9

Major 6th add 9th

(**Left** Hand)

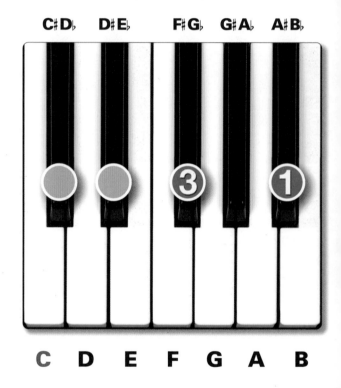

5 = little finger   4 = ring finger   3 = middle finger   2 = index finger   1 = thumb

Chord Spelling

1st (F#), 3rd (A#), 5th (C#), 6th (D#), 9th (G#)

F♯maj6/9
Major 6th add 9th
(**Right** Hand)

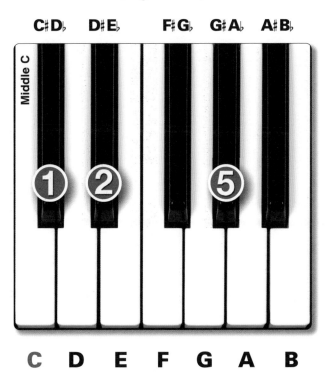

A
B♭/A♯
B
C
C♯/D♭
D
E♭/D♯
E
F
F♯/G♭
G
A♭/G♯
Other Chords

1 = thumb   2 = index finger   3 = middle finger   4 = ring finger   5 = little finger

Chord Spelling

1st (F♯), 3rd (C♯), 5th (C♯), 6th (D♯), 9th (G♯)

F#m6/9

Minor 6th add 9th

(**Left** Hand)

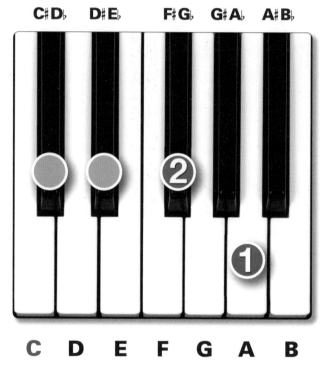

C#D♭　D#E♭　　F#G♭　G#A♭　A#B♭

C　D　E　F　G　A　B

5 = little finger   4 = ring finger   3 = middle finger   2 = index finger   1 = thumb

Chord Spelling

1st (F#), ♭3rd (A), 5th (C#), 6th (D#), 9th (G#)

F#m6/9

Minor 6th add 9th

(**Right** Hand)

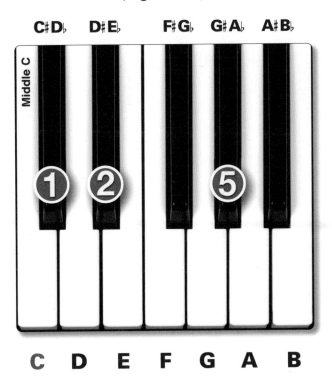

A

B♭/A#

B

C

C#/D♭

D

E♭/D#

E

F

F#/G♭

G

A♭/G#

Other Chords

1 = thumb 2 = index finger 3 = middle finger 4 = ring finger 5 = little finger

Chord Spelling

1st (F#), ♭3rd (A), 5th (C#), 6th (D#), 9th (G#)

F#6sus4

6th Suspended 4th

(**Left** Hand)

5 = little finger   4 = ring finger   3 = middle finger   2 = index finger   1 = thumb

Chord Spelling

1st (F#), 4th (B), 5th (C#), 6th (D#)

F#6sus4

6th Suspended 4th

(**Right** Hand)

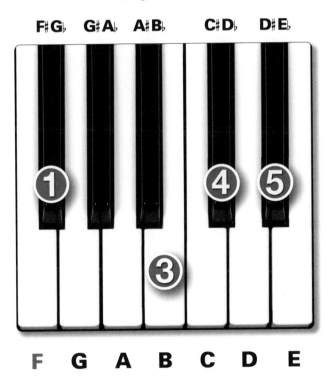

F#G♭　G#A♭　A#B♭　　C#D♭　　D#E♭

F　G　A　B　C　D　E

A
B♭/A#
B
C
C#/D♭
D
E♭/D#
E
F
F#/G♭
G
A♭/G#
Other Chords

1 = thumb　2 = index finger　3 = middle finger　4 = ring finger　5 = little finger

Chord Spelling

1st (F#), 4th (B), 5th (C#), 6th (D#)

F#maj7+5

Major 7th Augmented 5th

(Left Hand)

C#D♭   D#E♭   F#G♭   G#A♭   A#B♭

C   D   E   F   G   A   B

5 = little finger   4 = ring finger   3 = middle finger   2 = index finger   1 = thumb

Chord Spelling

1st (F#), 3rd (A#), #5th (Cx), 7th (E#)

A

B♭/A#

B

C

C#/D♭

D

E♭/D#

E

F

F#/G♭

G

A♭/G#

Other Chords

F#maj7 + 5

Major 7th Augmented 5th

(**Right** Hand)

C#D♭   D#E♭   F#G♭   G#A♭   A#B♭

Middle C

①   ③

C   D   E   F   G   A   B

1 = thumb   2 = index finger   3 = middle finger   4 = ring finger   5 = little finger

Chord Spelling

1st (F#), 3rd (A#), #5th (Cx), 7th (E#)

A

B♭/A#

B

C

C#/D♭

D

E♭/D#

E

F

F#/G♭

G

A♭/G#

Other Chords

F#maj7sus4

Major 7th Suspended 4th

(**Left** Hand)

C#D♭   D#E♭   F#G♭   G#A♭   A#B♭

C   D   E   F   G   A   B

5 = little finger   4 = ring finger   3 = middle finger   2 = index finger   1 = thumb

Chord Spelling

1st (F#), 4th (B), 5th (C#), 7th (E#)

F#maj7sus4

Major 7th Suspended 4th

(**Right** Hand)

1 = thumb   2 = index finger   3 = middle finger   4 = ring finger   5 = little finger

Chord Spelling

1st (F#), 4th (B), 5th (C#), 7th (E#)

A
Bb/A#
B
C
C#/Db
D
Eb/D#
E
F
F#/Gb
G
Ab/G#
Other Chords

F#m-maj7

Minor-Major 7th

(**Left** Hand)

5 = little finger   4 = ring finger   3 = middle finger   2 = index finger   1 = thumb

Chord Spelling

1st (F#), b3rd (A), 5th (C#), 7th (E#)

F#m-maj7
Minor-Major 7th
(**Right** Hand)

C#D♭   D#E♭   F#G♭   G#A♭   A#B♭

Middle C

①

④

C   D   E   F   G   A   B

1 = thumb   2 = index finger   3 = middle finger   4 = ring finger   5 = little finger

A
B♭/A#
B
C
C#/D♭
D
E♭/D#
E
F
F#/G♭
G
A♭/G#
Other Chords

Chord Spelling

1st (F#), ♭3rd (A), 5th (C#), 7th (E#)

F♯maj9

Major 9th

(**Left** Hand)

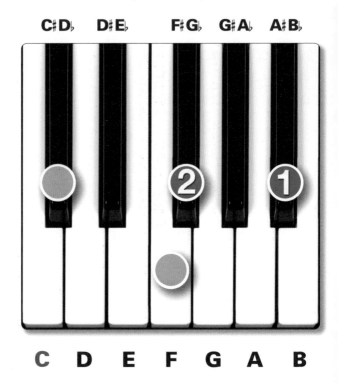

C♯D♭   D♯E♭   F♯G♭   G♯A♭   A♯B♭

C   D   E   F   G   A   B

5 = little finger   4 = ring finger   3 = middle finger   2 = index finger   1 = thumb

Chord Spelling

1st (F♯), 3rd (A♯), 5th (C♯), 7th (E♯), 9th (G♯)

F#maj9

Major 9th

(Right Hand)

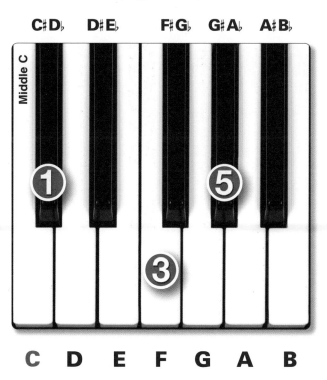

C#D♭ D#E♭ F#G♭ G#A♭ A#B♭

Middle C

① ⑤

③

C D E F G A B

A
B♭/A#
B
C
C#/D♭
D
E♭/D#
E
F
F#/G♭
G
A♭/G#
Other Chords

1 = thumb 2 = index finger 3 = middle finger 4 = ring finger 5 = little finger

Chord Spelling

1st (F#), 3rd (A#), 5th (C#), 7th (E#), 9th (G#)

F#m9

Minor 9th

(**Left** Hand)

C#D♭   D#E♭   F#G♭   G#A♭   A#B♭

C   D   E   F   G   A   B

5 = little finger   4 = ring finger   3 = middle finger   2 = index finger   1 = thumb

Chord Spelling

1st (F#), ♭3rd (A), 5th (C#), ♭7th (E), 9th (G#)

F♯m9

Minor 9th

(Right Hand)

C♯D♭   D♯E♭   F♯G♭   G♯A♭   A♯B♭

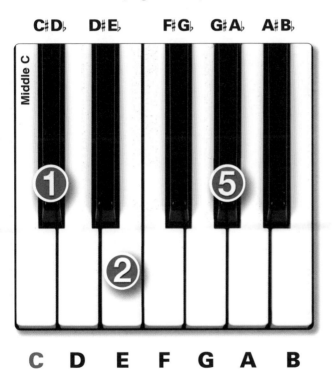

Middle C

C   D   E   F   G   A   B

1 = thumb   2 = index finger   3 = middle finger   4 = ring finger   5 = little finger

Chord Spelling

1st (F♯), ♭3rd (A), 5th (C♯), ♭7th (E), 9th (G♯)

A

B♭/A♯

B

C

C♯/D♭

D

E♭/D♯

E

F

F♯/G♭

G

A♭/G♯

Other Chords

F#m-maj9

Minor-Major 9th

(**Left** Hand)

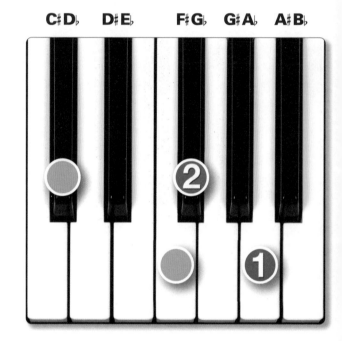

5 = little finger   4 = ring finger   3 = middle finger   2 = index finger   1 = thumb

Chord Spelling

1st (F#), ♭3rd (A), 5th (C#), 7th (E#), 9th (G#)

F#m-maj9

Minor-Major 9th

(**Right** Hand)

C#D♭   D#E♭   F#G♭   G#A♭   A#B♭

Middle C

① ③ ⑤

C   D   E   F   G   A   B

1 = thumb   2 = index finger   3 = middle finger   4 = ring finger   5 = little finger

Chord Spelling

1st (F#), ♭3rd (A), 5th (C#), 7th (E#), 9th (G#)

A

B♭/A#

B

C

C#/D♭

D

E♭/D#

E

F

F#/G♭

G

A♭/G#

Other Chords

F#maj11

Major 11th

(**Left** Hand)

5 = little finger   4 = ring finger   3 = middle finger   2 = index finger   1 = thumb

Chord Spelling

1st (F#), 3rd (A#), 5th (C#), 7th (E#),
9th (G#), 11th (B)

F#maj11
Major 11th
(**Right** Hand)

C#D♭ D#E♭ F#G♭ G#A♭ A#B♭

Middle C

C D E F G A B

1 = thumb   2 = index finger   3 = middle finger   4 = ring finger   5 = little finger

Chord Spelling

1st (F#), 3rd (A#), 5th (C#), 7th (E#),
9th (G#), 11th (B)

A

B♭/A#

B

C

C#/D♭

D

E♭/D#

E

F

F#/G♭

G

A♭/G#

Other
Chords

F#m11

Minor 11th

(**Left** Hand)

C#D♭   D#E♭   F#G♭   G#A♭   A#B♭

C   D   E   F   G   A   B

5 = little finger   4 = ring finger   3 = middle finger   2 = index finger   1 = thumb

Chord Spelling

1st (F#), ♭3rd (A), 5th (C#), ♭7th (E),
9th (G#), 11th (B)

A

B♭/A#

B

C

C#/D♭

D

E♭/D#

E

F

F#/G♭

G

A♭/G#

Other
Chords

F#m11

Minor 11th

(**Right** Hand)

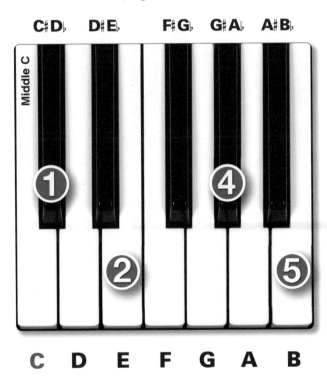

C♯D♭　D♯E♭　　F♯G♭　G♯A♭　A♯B♭

Middle C

① ④ ② ⑤

C D E F G A B

1 = thumb   2 = index finger   3 = middle finger   4 = ring finger   5 = little finger

A
B♭/A♯
B
C
C♯/D♭
D
E♭/D♯
E
F
F♯/G♭
G
A♭/G♯
Other Chords

Chord Spelling

1st (F♯), ♭3rd (A), 5th (C♯), ♭7th (E),
9th (G♯), 11th (B)

F#11

Dominant 11th

(**Left** Hand)

5 = little finger 4 = ring finger 3 = middle finger 2 = index finger 1 = thumb

Chord Spelling

1st (F#), 3rd (A#), 5th (C#), ♭7th (E),
9th (G#), 11th (B)

F♯11

Dominant 11th

(**Right** Hand)

C♯D♭ D♯E♭   F♯G♭ G♯A♭ A♯B♭

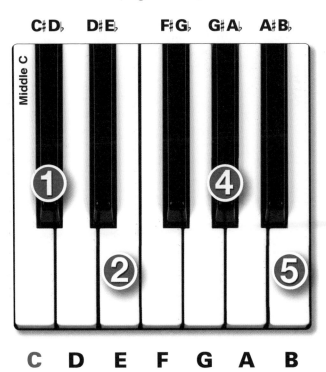

Middle C

C D E F G A B

1 = thumb   2 = index finger   3 = middle finger   4 = ring finger   5 = little finger

A

B♭/A♯

B

C

C♯/D♭

D

E♭/D♯

E

F

F♯/G♭

G

A♭/G♯

Other Chords

Chord Spelling

1st (F♯), 3rd (A♯), 5th (C♯), ♭7th (E),
9th (G♯), 11th (B)

F#maj13

Major 13th

(**Left** Hand)

F#G♭　　G#A♭　　A#B♭　　　C#D♭　　D#E♭

Middle C

⑤　　　　③　　　①

F　G　A　B　C　D　E

5 = little finger　4 = ring finger　3 = middle finger　2 = index finger　1 = thumb

Chord Spelling

1st (F#), 3rd (A#), 5th (C#), 7th (E#),
9th (G#), 11th (B), 13th (D#)

A

B♭/A#

B

C

C#/D♭

D

E♭/D#

E

F

F#/G♭

G

A♭/G#

Other
Chords

F#maj13

Major 13th

(**Right** Hand)

F#G♭ G#A♭ A#B♭   C#D♭ D#E♭

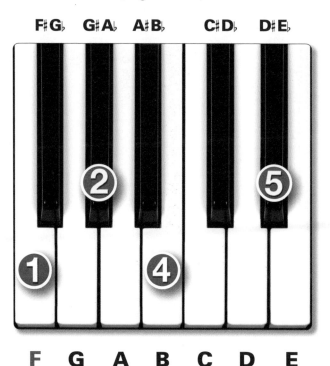

F G A B C D E

1 = thumb   2 = index finger   3 = middle finger   4 = ring finger   5 = little finger

A

B♭/A#

B

C

C#/D♭

D

E♭/D#

E

F

F#/G♭

G

A♭/G#

Other
Chords

Chord Spelling

1st (F#), 3rd (A#), 5th (C#), 7th (E#),
9th (G#), 11th (B), 13th (D#)

F#m13

Minor 13th

(**Left** Hand)

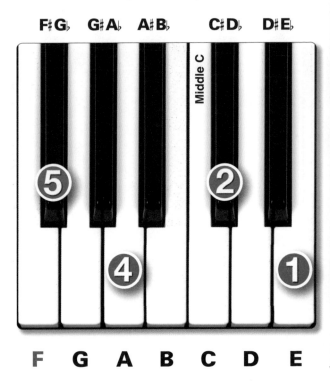

F#G♭ G#A♭ A#B♭   C#D♭   D#E♭

Middle C

F G A B C D E

5 = little finger   4 = ring finger   3 = middle finger   2 = index finger   1 = thumb

Chord Spelling

1st (F#), ♭3rd (A), 5th (C#), ♭7th (E),
9th (G#), 11th (B), 13th (D#)

A
B♭/A#
B
C
C#/D♭
D
E♭/D#
E
F
F#/G♭
G
A♭/G#
Other Chords

F#m13

Minor 13th

(**Right** Hand)

A

B♭/A#

B

C

C#/D♭

D

E♭/D#

E

F

F#/G♭

G

A♭/G#

Other Chords

F#G♭   G#A♭   A#B♭   C#D♭   D#E♭

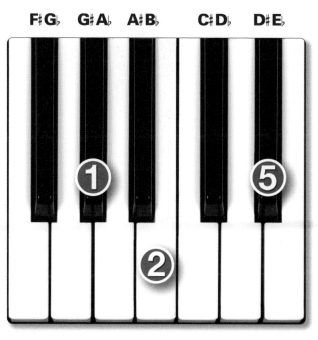

F   G   A   B   C   D   E

1 = thumb   2 = index finger   3 = middle finger   4 = ring finger   5 = little finger

Chord Spelling

1st (F#), ♭3rd (A), 5th (C#), ♭7th (E),
9th (G#), 11th (B), 13th (D#)

F#13

Dominant 13th

(**Left** Hand)

F#G♭ G#A♭ A#B♭   C#D♭ D#E♭

Middle C

⑤   ④   ②

①

F G A B C D E

5 = little finger 4 = ring finger 3 = middle finger 2 = index finger 1 = thumb

A
B♭/A#
B
C
C#/D♭
D
E♭/D#
E
F
F#/G♭
G
A♭/G#
Other Chords

Chord Spelling

1st (F#), 3rd (A#), 5th (C#), ♭7th (E),
9th (G#), 11th (B), 13th (D#)

F#13

Dominant 13th

(**Right** Hand)

A

B♭/A♯

B

C

C♯/D♭

D

E♭/D♯

E

F

F♯/G♭

G

A♭/G♯

Other Chords

F♯G♭   **G♯A♭**   **A♯B♭**   **C♯D♭**   **D♯E♭**

F   G   A   B   C   D   E

1 = thumb   2 = index finger   3 = middle finger   4 = ring finger   5 = little finger

Chord Spelling

1st (F♯), 3rd (A♯), 5th (C♯), ♭7th (E),
9th (G♯), 11th (B), 13th (D♯)

Gmaj6/9

Major 6th add 9th

(**Left** Hand)

C#D♭   D#E♭   F#G♭   G#A♭   A#B♭

C   D   E   F   G   A   B

5 = little finger   4 = ring finger   3 = middle finger   2 = index finger   1 = thumb

Chord Spelling

1st (G), 3rd (B), 5th (D), 6th (E), 9th (A)

Gmaj6/9

Major 6th add 9th

(**Right** Hand)

A

B♭/A♯

B

C

C♯/D♭

D

E♭/D♯

E

F

F♯/G♭

G

A♭/G♯

Other Chords

1 = thumb 2 = index finger 3 = middle finger 4 = ring finger 5 = little finger

Chord Spelling

1st (G), 3rd (B), 5th (D), 6th (E), 9th (A)

Gm6/9

Minor 6th add 9th

(**Left** Hand)

C#D♭   D#E♭   F#G♭   G#A♭   A#B♭

C   D   E   F   G   A   B

5 = little finger   4 = ring finger   3 = middle finger   2 = index finger   1 = thumb

Chord Spelling

1st (G), ♭3rd (B♭), 5th (D), 6th (E), 9th (A)

A

B♭/A#

B

C

C#/D♭

D

E♭/D#

E

F

F#/G♭

G

A♭/G#

Other Chords

Gm6/9

Minor 6th add 9th

(**Right** Hand)

C#D♭	D#E♭		F#G♭	G#A♭	A#B♭

Middle C

① ② ⑤

C D E F G A B

1 = thumb   2 = index finger   3 = middle finger   4 = ring finger   5 = little finger

Chord Spelling

1st (G), ♭3rd (B♭), 5th (D), 6th (E), 9th (A)

A

B♭/A#

B

C

C#/D♭

D

E♭/D#

E

F

F#/G♭

G

A♭/G#

Other Chords

G6sus4

6th Suspended 4th

(**Left** Hand)

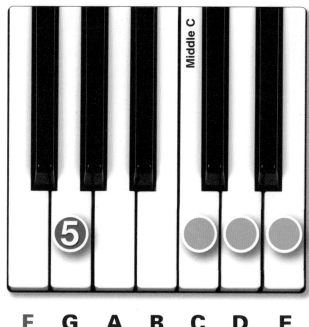

5 = little finger   4 = ring finger   3 = middle finger   2 = index finger   1 = thumb

Chord Spelling

1st (G), 4th (C), 5th (D), 6th (E)

G6sus4

6th Suspended 4th

(**Right** Hand)

F#G♭ G#A♭ A#B♭   C#D♭   D#E♭

① ③④⑤

F G A B C D E

A
B♭/A#
B
C
C#/D♭
D
E♭/D#
E
F
F#/G♭
G
A♭/G#
Other Chords

1 = thumb   2 = index finger   3 = middle finger   4 = ring finger   5 = little finger

Chord Spelling

1st (G), 4th (C), 5th (D), 6th (E)

Gmaj7+5

Major 7th Augmented 5th

(**Left** Hand)

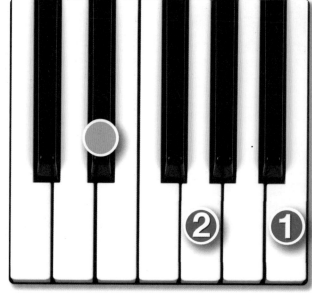

C#D♭   D#E♭   F#G♭   G#A♭   A#B♭

C   D   E   F   G   A   B

5 = little finger   4 = ring finger   3 = middle finger   2 = index finger   1 = thumb

Chord Spelling

1st (G), 3rd (B), #5th (D#), 7th (F#)

Gmaj7+5

Major 7th Augmented 5th

(**Right** Hand)

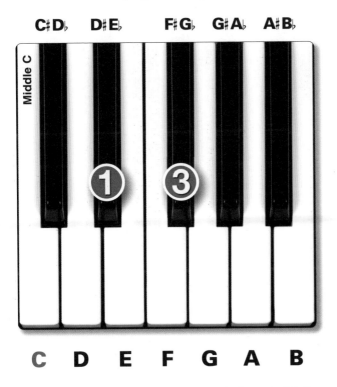

C#D♭ D#E♭ F#G♭ G#A♭ A#B♭

Middle C

① ③

C D E F G A B

1 = thumb 2 = index finger 3 = middle finger 4 = ring finger 5 = little finger

Chord Spelling

1st (G), 3rd (B), #5th (D#), 7th (F#)

A

B♭/A#

B

C

C#/D♭

D

E♭/D#

E

F

F#/G♭

G

A♭/G#

Other Chords

Gmaj7sus4

Major 7th Suspended 4th

(**Left** Hand)

C♯D♭ D♯E♭ F♯G♭ G♯A♭ A♯B♭

C D E F G A B

5 = little finger   4 = ring finger   3 = middle finger   2 = index finger   1 = thumb

Chord Spelling

1st (G), 4th (C), 5th (E), 7th (F♯)

Gmaj7sus4
Major 7th Suspended 4th

(**Right** Hand)

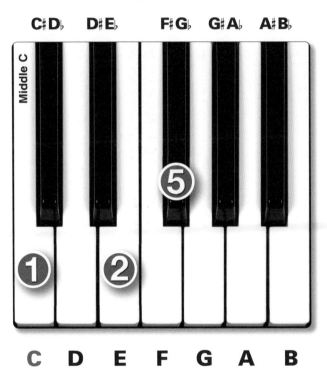

1 = thumb 2 = index finger 3 = middle finger 4 = ring finger 5 = little finger

Chord Spelling

1st (G), 4th (C), 5th (E), 7th (F#)

A
Bb/A#
B
C
C#/Db
D
Eb/D#
E
F
F#/Gb
G
Ab/G#
Other Chords

Gm-maj7
Minor-Major 7th
(**Left** Hand)

5 = little finger 4 = ring finger 3 = middle finger 2 = index finger 1 = thumb

Chord Spelling

1st (G), ♭3rd (B♭), 5th (D), 7th (F♯)

Gm-maj7

Minor-Major 7th

(**Right** Hand)

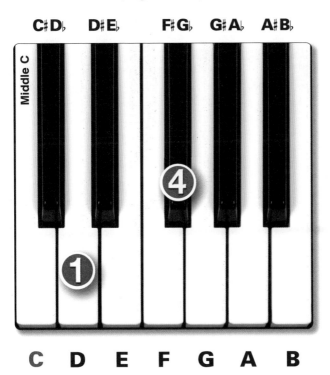

1 = thumb   2 = index finger   3 = middle finger   4 = ring finger   5 = little finger

Chord Spelling

1st (G), b3rd (Bb), 5th (D), 7th (F#)

Gmaj9

Major 9th

(**Left** Hand)

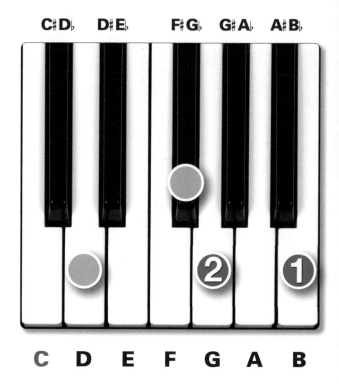

C♯D♭   D♯E♭   F♯G♭   G♯A♭   A♯B♭

C   D   E   F   G   A   B

5 = little finger   4 = ring finger   3 = middle finger   2 = index finger   1 = thumb

Chord Spelling

1st (G), 3rd (B), 5th (D), 7th (F♯), 9th (A)

Gmaj9
Major 9th
(**Right** Hand)

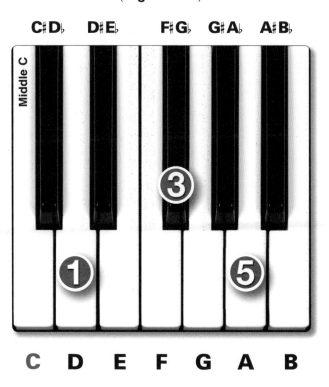

1 = thumb   2 = index finger   3 = middle finger   4 = ring finger   5 = little finger

Chord Spelling

1st (G), 3rd (B), 5th (D), 7th (F♯), 9th (A)

A
B♭/A♯
B
C
C♯/D♭
D
E♭/D♯
E
F
F♯/G♭
G
A♭/G♯
Other Chords

Gm9

Minor 9th

(**Left** Hand)

C♯D♭   D♯E♭   F♯G♭   G♯A♭   A♯B♭

C   D   E   F   G   A   B

5 = little finger   4 = ring finger   3 = middle finger   2 = index finger   1 = thumb

Chord Spelling

1st (G), ♭3rd (B♭), 5th (D), ♭7th (F), 9th (A)

Gm9

Minor 9th

(**Right** Hand)

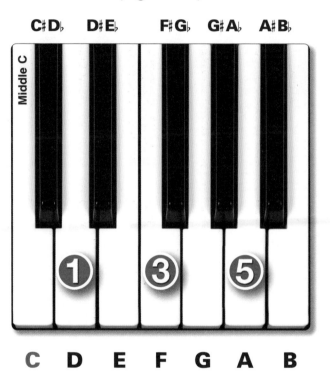

C#D♭   D#E♭   F#G♭   G#A♭   A#B♭

Middle C

① ③ ⑤

C   D   E   F   G   A   B

A
B♭/A#
B
C
C#/D♭
D
E♭/D#
E
F
F#/G♭
G
A♭/G#
Other Chords

1 = thumb   2 = index finger   3 = middle finger   4 = ring finger   5 = little finger

Chord Spelling

1st (G), ♭3rd (B♭), 5th (D), ♭7th (F), 9th (A)

Gm-maj9
Minor-Major 9th
(**Left** Hand)

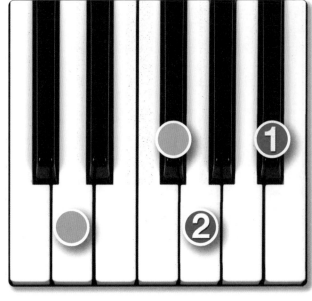

C#D♭   D#E♭   F#G♭   G#A♭   A#B♭

C   D   E   F   G   A   B

5 = little finger   4 = ring finger   3 = middle finger   2 = index finger   1 = thumb

Chord Spelling

1st (G), ♭3rd (B♭), 5th (D), 7th (F♯), 9th (A)

Gm-maj9
Minor-Major 9th

(**Right** Hand)

C#D♭   D#E♭   F#G♭   G#A♭   A#B♭

Middle C

③   ⑤

①   ⑤

C   D   E   F   G   A   B

1 = thumb   2 = index finger   3 = middle finger   4 = ring finger   5 = little finger

A
B♭/A#
B
C
C#/D♭
D
E♭/D#
E
F
F#/G♭
G
A♭/G#
Other Chords

Chord Spelling

1st (G), ♭3rd (B♭), 5th (D), 7th (F#), 9th (A)

Gmaj11

Major 11th

(**Left** Hand)

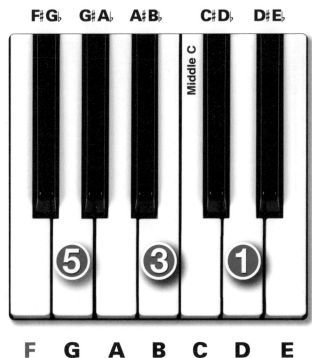

F♯G♭ G♯A♭ A♯B♭ C♯D♭ D♯E♭

Middle C

F G A B C D E

5 = little finger   4 = ring finger   3 = middle finger   2 = index finger   1 = thumb

Chord Spelling

1st (G), 3rd (B), 5th (D), 7th (F♯),
9th (A), 11th (C)

Gmaj11
Major 11th
(**Right** Hand)

F#G♭   G#A♭   A#B♭   C#D♭   D#E♭

F   G   A   B   C   D   E

A

B♭/A#

B

C

C#/D♭

D

E♭/D#

E

F

F#/G♭

G

A♭/G#

Other
Chords

1 = thumb   2 = index finger   3 = middle finger   4 = ring finger   5 = little finger

Chord Spelling

1st (G), 3rd (B), 5th (D), 7th (F#),
9th (A), 11th (C)

Gm11

Minor 11th

(**Left** Hand)

F#G♭   G#A♭   A#B♭   C#D♭   D#E♭

Middle C

F   G   A   B   C   D   E

5 = little finger   4 = ring finger   3 = middle finger   2 = index finger   1 = thumb

Chord Spelling

1st (G), ♭3rd (B♭), 5th (D), ♭7th (F),
9th (A), 11th (C)

Gm11

Minor 11th

(**Right** Hand)

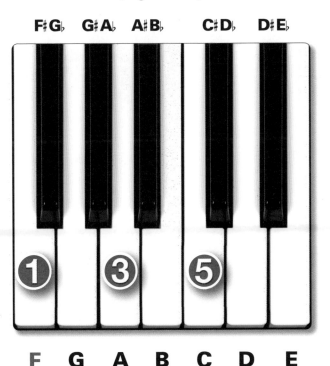

F#G♭ G#A♭ A#B♭ C#D♭ D#E♭

F G A B C D E

A
B♭/A#
B
C
C#/D♭
D
E♭/D#
E
F
F#/G♭
G
A♭/G#
Other Chords

1 = thumb   2 = index finger   3 = middle finger   4 = ring finger   5 = little finger

Chord Spelling

1st (G), ♭3rd (B♭), 5th (D), ♭7th (F),
9th (A), 11th (C)

A

B♭/A♯

B

C

C♯/D♭

D

E♭/D♯

E

F

F♯/G♭

G

A♭/G♯

Other
Chords

G11

Dominant 11th

(**Left** Hand)

F♯G♭   G♯A♭   A♯B♭   C♯D♭   D♯E♭

Middle C

⑤   ③   ①

F   G   A   B   C   D   E

5 = little finger   4 = ring finger   3 = middle finger   2 = index finger   1 = thumb

Chord Spelling

1st (G), 3rd (B), 5th (D), ♭7th (F),
9th (A), 11th (C)

G11

Dominant 11th

(**Right** Hand)

A
B♭/A♯
B
C
C♯/D♭
D
E♭/D♯
E
F
F♯/G♭
G
A♭/G♯
Other Chords

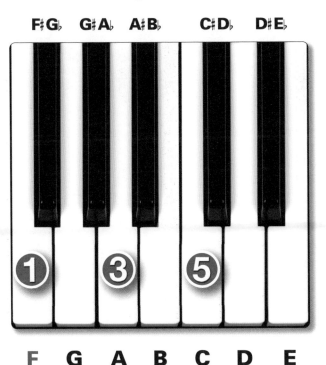

F♯G♭ G♯A♭ A♯B♭   C♯D♭   D♯E♭

1   **3**   **5**

F   G   A   B   C   D   E

1 = thumb   2 = index finger   3 = middle finger   4 = ring finger   5 = little finger

Chord Spelling

1st (G), 3rd (D), 5th (D), ♭7th (F),
9th (A), 11th (C)

Fmaj13

Major 13th

(**Left** Hand)

F#G♭ G#A♭ A#B♭   C#D♭ D#E♭

Middle C

⑤   ③   ①

F G A B C D E

5 = little finger 4 = ring finger 3 = middle finger 2 = index finger 1 = thumb

A
B♭/A#
B
C
C#/D♭
D
E♭/D#
E
F
F#/G♭
G
A♭/G#
Other Chords

Chord Spelling

1st (G), 3rd (B), 5th (D), 7th (F#),
9th (A), 11th (C), 13th (E)

Fmaj13
Major 13th
(**Right** Hand)

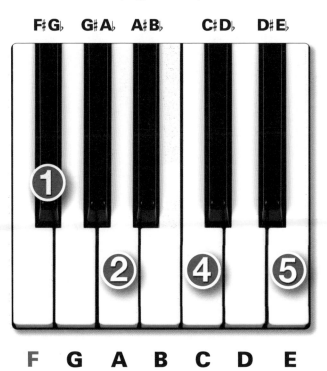

F#G♭ G#A♭ A#B♭   C#D♭   D#E♭

F G A B C D E

A

B♭/A#

B

C

C#/D♭

D

E♭/D#

E

F

F#/G♭

G

A♭/G#

Other Chords

1 = thumb   2 = index finger   3 = middle finger   4 = ring finger   5 = little finger

Chord Spelling

1st (G), 3rd (B), 5th (D), 7th (F#),
9th (A), 11th (C), 13th (E)

Fm13
Minor 13th
(**Left** Hand)

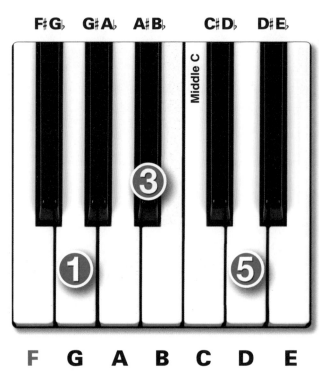

F#G♭ G#A♭ A#B♭   C#D♭ D#E♭

Middle C

③

①   ⑤

F   G   A   B   C   D   E

5 = little finger   4 = ring finger   3 = middle finger   2 = index finger   1 = thumb

A

B♭/A#

B

C

C#/D♭

D

E♭/D#

E

F

F#/G♭

G

A♭/G#

Other Chords

Chord Spelling

1st (G), ♭3rd (B♭), 5th (D), ♭7th (F),
9th (A), 11th (C), 13th (E)

Fm13
Minor 13th

(Right Hand)

F#G♭ G#A♭ A#B♭   C#D♭   D#E♭

① ② ④ ⑤

F G A B C D E

A
B♭/A#
B
C
C#/D♭
D
E♭/D#
E
F
F#/G♭
G
A♭/G#
Other Chords

1 = thumb   2 = index finger   3 = middle finger   4 = ring finger   5 = little finger

Chord Spelling

1st (G), ♭3rd (B♭), 5th (D), ♭7th (F),
9th (A), 11th (C), 13th (E)

G13

Dominant 13th

(**Left** Hand)

F♯G♭ G♯A♭ A♯B♭   C♯D♭ D♯E♭

Middle C

⑤   ③   ①

F   G   A   B   C   D   E

A
B♭/A♯
B
C
C♯/D♭
D
E♭/D♯
E
F
F♯/G♭
G
A♭/G♯
Other Chords

5 = little finger   4 = ring finger   3 = middle finger   2 = index finger   1 = thumb

Chord Spelling

1st (G), 3rd (B), 5th (D), ♭7th (F),
9th (A), 11th (C), 13th (E)

G13

Dominant 13th

(**Right** Hand)

F♯G♭   **G♯A♭**   **A♯B♭**   **C♯D♭**   **D♯E♭**

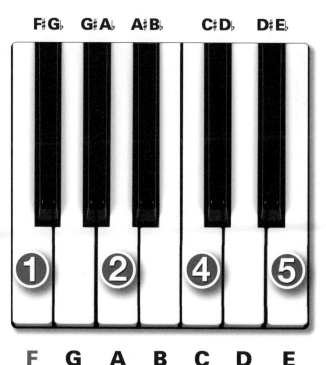

F   G   A   B   C   D   E

1 = thumb   2 = index finger   3 = middle finger   4 = ring finger   5 = little finger

Chord Spelling

1st (G), 3rd (B), 5th (D), ♭7th (F),
9th (A), 11th (C), 13th (E)

A

B♭/A♯

B

C

C♯/D♭

D

E♭/D♯

E

F

F♯/G♭

G

A♭/G♯

Other Chords

A♭maj6/9

Major 6th add 9th

(**Left** Hand)

5 = little finger 4 = ring finger 3 = middle finger 2 = index finger 1 = thumb

Chord Spelling

1st (A♭), 3rd (C), 5th (E♭), 6th (F), 9th (B♭)

Sidebar navigation:

A
B♭/A♯
B
C
C♯/D♭
D
E♭/D♯
E
F
F♯/G♭
G
A♭/G♯
Other Chords

A♭maj6/9
Major 6th add 9th

(**Right** Hand)

A
B♭/A♯
B
C
C♯/D♭
D
E♭/D♯
E
F
F♯/G♭
G
A♭/G♯
Other Chords

C♯D♭   D♯E♭   F♯G♭   G♯A♭   A♯B♭

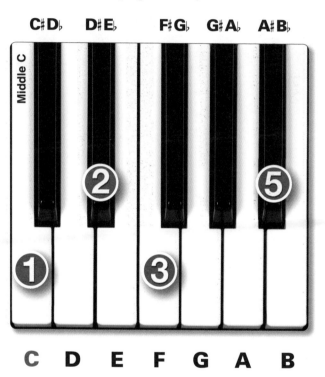

Middle C

C D E F G A B

1 = thumb   2 = index finger   3 = middle finger   4 = ring finger   5 = little finger

Chord Spelling

1st (A♭), 3rd (C), 5th (E♭), 6th (F), 9th (B♭)

A♭m6/9
Minor 6th add 9th
(**Left** Hand)

C♯D♭   D♯E♭   F♯G♭   G♯A♭   A♯B♭

C   D   E   F   G   A   B

5 = little finger   4 = ring finger   3 = middle finger   2 = index finger   1 = thumb

Chord Spelling

1st (A♭), ♭3rd (C♭), 5th (E♭), 6th (F), 9th (B♭)

A

B♭/A♯

B

C

C♯/D♭

D

E♭/D♯

E

F

F♯/G♭

G

A♭/G♯

Other Chords

A♭m6/9

Minor 6th add 9th

(**Right** Hand)

C♯D♭   D♯E♭   F♯G♭   G♯A♭   A♯B♭

Middle C

C   D   E   F   G   A   B

1 = thumb   2 = index finger   3 = middle finger   4 = ring finger   5 = little finger

A
B♭/A♯
B
C
C♯/D♭
D
E♭/D♯
E
F
F♯/G♭
G
A♭/G♯
Other Chords

Chord Spelling

1st (A♭), ♭3rd (C♭), 5th (E♭), 6th (F), 9th (B♭)

A♭6sus4

6th Suspended 4th

(**Left** Hand)

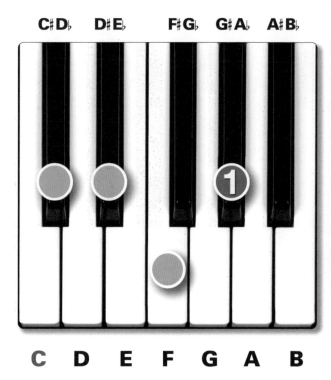

C#D♭   D#E♭   F#G♭ G#A♭ A#B♭

C   D   E   F   G   A   B

5 = little finger   4 = ring finger   3 = middle finger   2 = index finger   1 = thumb

Chord Spelling

1st (A♭), 4th (D♭), 5th (E♭), 6th (F)

A♭6sus4

6th Suspended 4th

(**Right** Hand)

1 = thumb   2 = index finger   3 = middle finger   4 = ring finger   5 = little finger

Chord Spelling

1st (A♭), 4th (D♭), 5th (E♭), 6th (F)

A

B♭/A♯

B

C

C♯/D♭

D

E♭/D♯

E

F

F♯/G♭

G

A♭/G♯

Other Chords

A

Bb/A#

B

C

C#/Db

D

Eb/D#

E

F

F#/Gb

G

Ab/G#

Other
Chords

A♭maj7+5

Major 7th Augmented 5th

(**Left** Hand)

C#D♭　　D#E♭　　　F#G♭　　G#A♭　　A#B♭

C　D　E　F　G　A　B

5 = little finger　4 = ring finger　3 = middle finger　2 = index finger　1 = thumb

Chord Spelling

1st (A♭), 3rd (C), #5th (E), 7th (F)

A♭maj7+5

Major 7th Augmented 5th

(**Right** Hand)

A
B♭/A♯
B
C
C♯/D♭
D
E♭/D♯
E
F
F♯/G♭
G
A♭/G♯
Other Chords

C#D♭ D#E♭   F#G♭ G#A♭ A#B♭

Middle C

C D E F G A B

1 = thumb   2 = index finger   3 = middle finger   4 = ring finger   5 = little finger

Chord Spelling

1st (A♭), 3rd (C), ♯5th (E), 7th (F)

A♭maj7sus4

Major 7th Suspended 4th

(**Left** Hand)

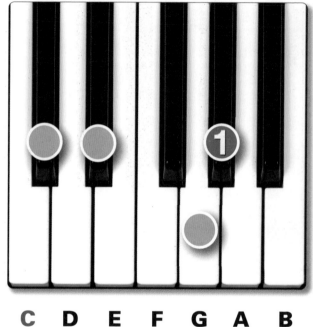

C#D♭ D#E♭   F#G♭ G#A♭ A#B♭

C D E F G A B

5 = little finger 4 = ring finger 3 = middle finger 2 = index finger 1 = thumb

Chord Spelling

1st (A♭), 4th (D♭), 5th (E♭), 7th (G)

A♭maj7sus4
Major 7th Suspended 4th

(**Right** Hand)

1 = thumb   2 = index finger   3 = middle finger   4 = ring finger   5 = little finger

Chord Spelling

1st (A♭), 4th (D♭), 5th (E♭), 7th (G)

A
B♭/A♯
B
C
C♯/D♭
D
E♭/D♯
E
F
F♯/G♭
G
A♭/G♯
Other Chords

A♭m-maj7
Minor-Major 7th
(**Left** Hand)

C#D♭   D#E♭   F#G♭   G#A♭   A#B♭

C D E F G A B

5 = little finger   4 = ring finger   3 = middle finger   2 = index finger   1 = thumb

Chord Spelling

1st (A♭), ♭3rd (C♭), 5th (E♭), 7th (G♭)

A

B♭/A#

B

C

C#/D♭

D

E♭/D#

E

F

F#/G♭

G

A♭/G#

Other Chords

A♭m-maj7
Minor-Major 7th
(**Right** Hand)

A

B♭/A♯

B

C

C♯/D♭

D

E♭/D♯

E

F

F♯/G♭

G

A♭/G♯

Other Chords

C♯D♭   D♯E♭   F♯G♭   G♯A♭   A♯B♭

Middle C

① ③

C D E F G A B

1 = thumb   2 = index finger   3 = middle finger   4 = ring finger   5 = little finger

Chord Spelling

1st (A♭), ♭3rd (C♭), 5th (E♭), 7th (G♭)

A♭maj9

Major 9th

(**Left** Hand)

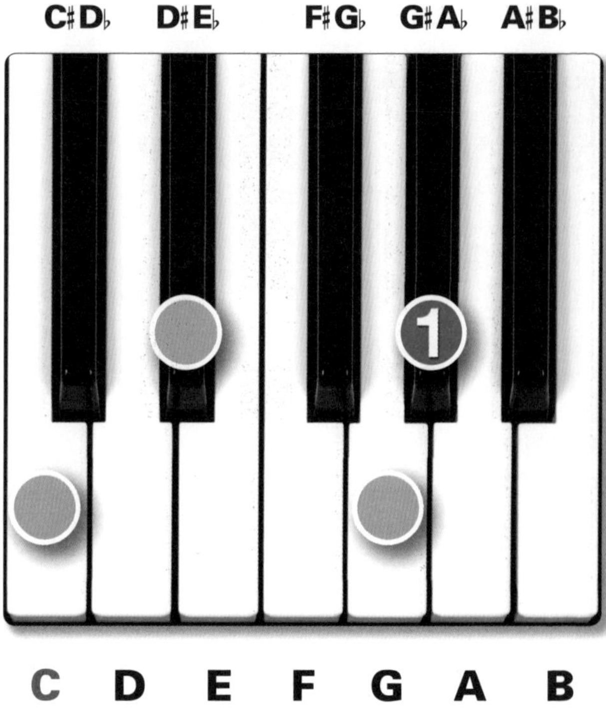

C#D♭ D#E♭ F#G♭ G#A♭ A#B♭

C D E F G A B

5 = little finger 4 = ring finger 3 = middle finger 2 = index finger 1 = thumb

Chord Spelling

1st (A♭), 3rd (C), 5th (E♭), 7th (G), 9th (B♭)

A♭maj9

Major 9th

(**Right** Hand)

A

B♭/A♯

B

C

C♯/D♭

D

E♭/D♯

E

F

F♯/G♭

G

A♭/G♯

Other Chords

C♯ D♭   D♯ E♭   F♯ G♭   G♯ A♭   A♯ B♭

Middle C

C   D   E   F   G   A   B

1 = thumb   2 = index finger   3 = middle finger   4 = ring finger   5 = little finger

Chord Spelling

1st (A♭), 3rd (C), 5th (E♭), 7th (G), 9th (B♭)

A♭m9

Minor 9th

(**Left** Hand)

C#D♭   D#E♭   F#G♭   G#A♭   A#B♭

C   D   E   F   G   A   B

5 = little finger   4 = ring finger   3 = middle finger   2 = index finger   1 = thumb

Chord Spelling

1st (A♭), ♭3rd (C♭), 5th (E♭), ♭7th (G♭), 9th (B♭)

A
B♭/A#
B
C
C#/D♭
D
E♭/D#
E
F
F#/G♭
G
A♭/G#
Other Chords

A♭m9

Minor 9th

(**Right** Hand)

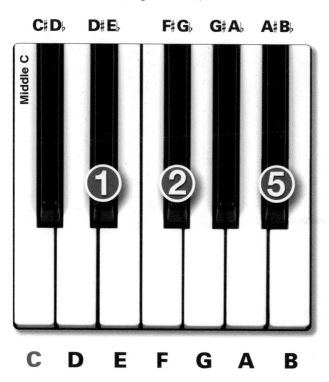

C#D♭   D#E♭   F#G♭   G#A♭   A#B♭

Middle C

① ② ⑤

C D E F G A B

1 = thumb   2 = index finger   3 = middle finger   4 = ring finger   5 = little finger

Chord Spelling

1st (A♭), ♭3rd (C♭), 5th (E♭), ♭7th (G♭), 9th (B♭)

A

B♭/A#

B

C

C#/D♭

D

E♭/D#

E

F

F#/G♭

G

A♭/G#

Other Chords

A♭m-maj9

Minor-Major 9th

(**Left** Hand)

C♯D♭ D♯E♭ F♯G♭ G♯A♭ A♯B♭

C D E F G A B

5 = little finger   4 = ring finger   3 = middle finger   2 = index finger   1 = thumb

Chord Spelling

1st (A♭), ♭3rd (C♭), 5th (E♭), 7th (G), 9th (B♭)

A♭m-maj9

Minor-Major 9th

(**Right** Hand)

1 = thumb   2 = index finger   3 = middle finger   4 = ring finger   5 = little finger

Chord Spelling

1st (A♭), ♭3rd (C♭), 5th (E♭), 7th (G), 9th (B♭)

A

B♭/A♯

B

C

C♯/D♭

D

E♭/D♯

E

F

F♯/G♭

G

A♭/G♯

Other Chords

A♭maj11

Major 11th

(**Left** Hand)

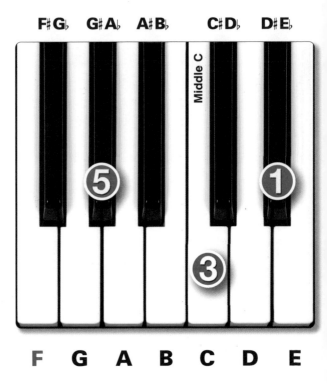

F♯G♭   G♯A♭   A♯B♭   C♯D♭   D♯E♭

Middle C

⑤   ①
                ③

F   G   A   B   C   D   E

5 = little finger   4 = ring finger   3 = middle finger   2 = index finger   1 = thumb

Chord Spelling

1st (A♭), 3rd (C), 5th (E♭), 7th (G),
9th (B♭), 11th (D♭)

A

B♭/A♯

B

C

C♯/D♭

D

E♭/D♯

E

F

F♯/G♭

G

A♭/G♯

Other Chords

A♭maj11

Major 11th

(**Right** Hand)

F#G♭ G#A♭ A#B♭ C#D♭ D#E♭

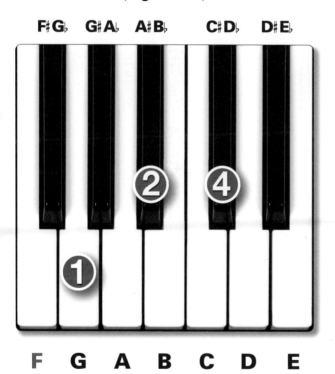

F G A B C D E

1 = thumb   2 = index finger   3 = middle finger   4 = ring finger   5 = little finger

Chord Spelling

1st (A♭), 3rd (C), 5th (E♭), 7th (G),
9th (B♭), 11th (D♭)

A
B♭/A#
B
C
C#/D♭
D
E♭/D#
E
F
F#/G♭
G
A♭/G#
Other Chords

A♭m11

Minor 11th

(**Left** Hand)

F#G♭ G#A♭ A#B♭ C#D♭ D#E♭

Middle C

⑤ ③ ①

F G A B C D E

5 = little finger   4 = ring finger   3 = middle finger   2 = index finger   1 = thumb

Chord Spelling

1st (A♭), ♭3rd (C♭), 5th (E♭), ♭7th (G♭),
9th (B♭), 11th (D♭)

A
B♭/A#
B
C
C#/D♭
D
E♭/D#
E
F
F#/G♭
G
A♭/G#
Other Chords

A♭m11

Minor 11th

(**Right** Hand)

F#G♭   G#A♭   A#B♭   C#D♭   D#E♭

F   G   A   B   C   D   E

1 = thumb   2 = index finger   3 = middle finger   4 = ring finger   5 = little finger

Chord Spelling

1st (A♭), ♭3rd (C♭), 5th (E♭), ♭7th (G♭),
9th (B♭), 11th (D♭)

A

B♭/A#

B

C

C#/D♭

D

E♭/D#

E

F

F#/G♭

G

A♭/G#

Other Chords

A♭11

Dominant 11th

(**Left** Hand)

F♯G♭   G♯A♭   A♯B♭   C♯D♭   D♯E♭

Middle C

F   G   A   B   C   D   E

5 = little finger   4 = ring finger   3 = middle finger   2 = index finger   1 = thumb

Chord Spelling

1st (A♭), 3rd (C), 5th (E♭), ♭7th (G♭),
9th (B♭), 11th (D♭)

A

B♭/A♯

B

C

C♯/D♭

D

E♭/D♯

E

F

F♯/G♭

G

A♭/G♯

Other
Chords

A♭11

Dominant 11th

(**Right** Hand)

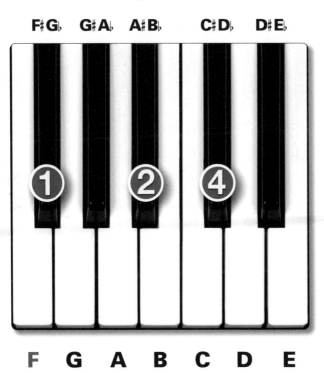

F#G♭ G#A♭ A#B♭   C#D♭   D#E♭

F   G   A   B   C   D   E

1 = thumb   2 = index finger   3 = middle finger   4 = ring finger   5 = little finger

A

B♭/A#

B

C

C#/D♭

D

E♭/D#

E

F

F#/G♭

G

A♭/G#

Other Chords

Chord Spelling

1st (A♭), 3rd (C), 5th (E♭), ♭7th (G♭),
9th (B♭), 11th (D♭)

A♭maj13
Major 13th
(**Left** Hand)

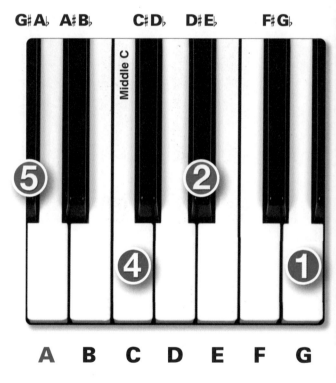

G♯A♭ A♯B♭   C♯D♭   D♯E♭   F♯G♭

Middle C

A B C D E F G

5 = little finger   4 = ring finger   3 = middle finger   2 = index finger   1 = thumb

Chord Spelling

1st (A♭), 3rd (C), 5th (E♭), 7th (G),
9th (B♭), 11th (D♭), 13th (F)

A♭maj13
Major 13th
(**Right** Hand)

G♯A♭ A♯B♭   C♯D♭   D♯E♭   F♯G♭

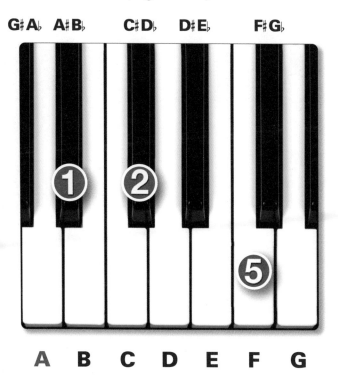

A   B   C   D   E   F   G

1 = thumb   2 = index finger   3 = middle finger   4 = ring finger   5 = little finger

Chord Spelling

1st (A♭), 3rd (C), 5th (E♭), 7th (G),
9th (B♭), 11th (D♭), 13th (F)

A

B♭/A♯

B

C

C♯/D♭

D

E♭/D♯

E

F

F♯/G♭

G

A♭/G♯

Other Chords

A♭m13

Minor 13th

(**Left** Hand)

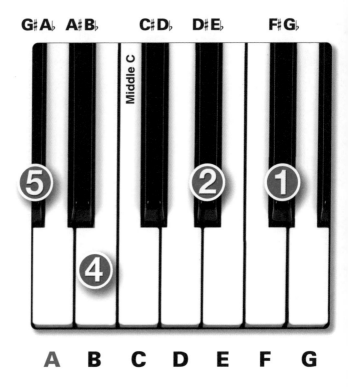

5 = little finger   4 = ring finger   3 = middle finger   2 = index finger   1 = thumb

Chord Spelling

1st (A♭), ♭3rd (C♭), 5th (E♭), ♭7th (G♭),
9th (B♭), 11th (D♭), 13th (F)

A♭m13

Minor 13th

(**Right** Hand)

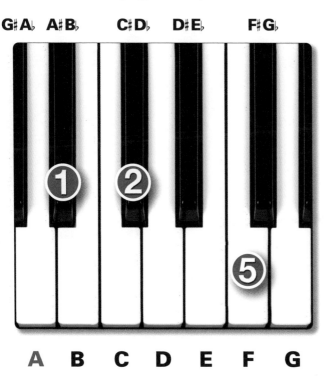

1 = thumb   2 = index finger   3 = middle finger   4 = ring finger   5 = little finger

Chord Spelling

1st (A♭), ♭3rd (C♭), 5th (E♭), ♭7th (G♭),
9th (B♭), 11th (D♭), 13th (F)

A
B♭/A#
B
C
C#/D♭
D
E♭/D#
E
F
F#/G♭
G
A♭/G#
Other Chords

A♭13

Dominant 13th

(**Left** Hand)

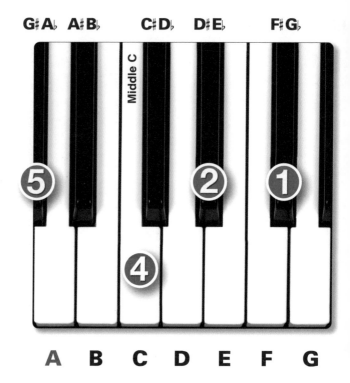

5 = little finger   4 = ring finger   3 = middle finger   2 = index finger   1 = thumb

Chord Spelling

1st (A♭), 3rd (C), 5th (E♭), ♭7th (G♭),
9th (B♭), 11th (D♭), 13th (F)

A♭13

Dominant 13th

(**Right** Hand)

A

B♭/A♯

B

C

C♯/D♭

D

E♭/D♯

E

F

F♯/G♭

G

A♭/G♯

Other Chords

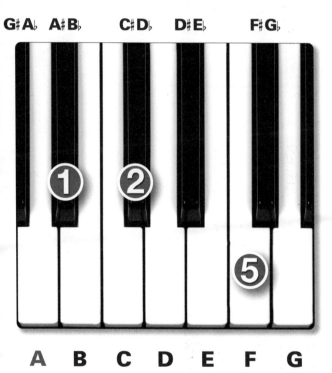

G♯A♭ A♯B♭   C♯D♭   D♯E♭   F♯G♭

A   B   C   D   E   F   G

1 = thumb   2 = index finger   3 = middle finger   4 = ring finger   5 = little finger

Chord Spelling

1st (A♭), 3rd (C), 5th (E♭), ♭7th (G♭),
9th (B♭), 11th (D♭), 13th (F)

First Inversions – Major 6th add 9th

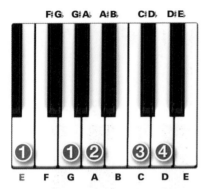

Cmaj6/9
C Major 6th add 9t
(1st inversion: 3rd as bass no

Chord Spelling
3rd (E), 5th (G), 6th (A),
1st (C), 9th (D)

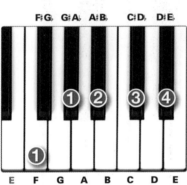

C♯maj6/9
C♯ Major 6th add 9t
(1st inversion: 3rd as bass no

Chord Spelling
3rd (E♯), 5th (G♯), 6th (A)♯
1st (C♯), 9th (D♯)

Dmaj6/9
D Major 6th add 9t
(1st inversion: 3rd as bass no

Chord Spelling
3rd (F♯), 5th (A), 6th (B),
1st (D), 9th (E)

First Inversions – Major 6th add 9th

E♭maj6/9

♭ Major 6th add 9th
(1st inversion: 3rd as bass note)

Chord Spelling
3rd (G), 5th (B♭), 6th (C),
1st (E♭), 9th (F)

Emaj6/9

E Major 6th add 9th
(1st inversion: 3rd as bass note)

Chord Spelling
3rd (G♯), 5th (B), 6th (C♯),
1st (E), 9th (F♯)

Fmaj6/9

F Major 6th add 9th
(1st inversion: 3rd as bass note)

Chord Spelling
3rd (A), 5th (C), 6th (D),
1st (F), 9th (G)

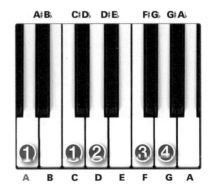

First Inversions – Major 6th add 9th

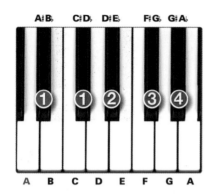

F#maj6/9
F# Major 6th add 9th
(1st inversion: 3rd as bass note)

Chord Spelling
3rd (A#), 5th (C#), 6th (D#),
1st (F#), 9th (G#)

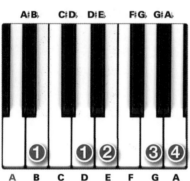

Gmaj6/9
G Major 6th add 9th
(1st inversion: 3rd as bass note)

Chord Spelling
3rd (B), 5th (D), 6th (E),
1st (G), 9th (A)

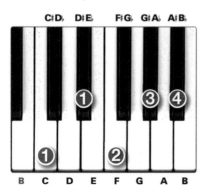

Abmaj6/9
Ab Major 6th add 9th
(1st inversion: 3rd as bass note)

Chord Spelling
3rd (C), 5th (Eb), 6th (F),
1st (Ab), 9th (Bb)

First Inversions – Major 6th add 9th

Amaj6/9
A Major 6th add 9th
(1st inversion: 3rd as bass note)

Chord Spelling
3rd (C♯), 5th (E), 6th (F♯),
1st (A), 9th (B)

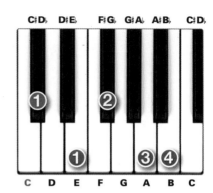

B♭maj6/9
B♭ Major 6th add 9th
(1st inversion: 3rd as bass note)

Chord Spelling
3rd (D), 5th (F), 6th (G),
1st (B♭), 9th (C)

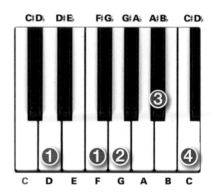

Bmaj6/9
B Major 6th add 9th
(1st inversion: 3rd as bass note)

Chord Spelling
3rd (D♯), 5th (F♯), 6th (G♯),
1st (B), 9th (C♯)

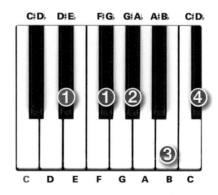

First Inversions – Minor 6th add 9th

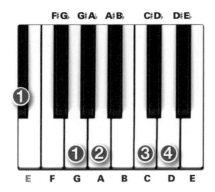

Cm6/9
C Minor 6th add 9th
(1st inversion: 3rd as bass note)

Chord Spelling
♭3rd (E♭), 5th (G), 6th (A),
1st (C), 9th (D)

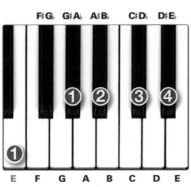

C#m6/9
C# Minor 6th add 9th
(1st inversion: 3rd as bass note)

Chord Spelling
♭3rd (E), 5th (G#), 6th (A#),
1st (C#), 9th (D#)

Dm6/9
D Minor 6th add 9th
(1st inversion: 3rd as bass note)

Chord Spelling
♭3rd (F), 5th (A), 6th (B),
1st (D), 9th (E)

First Inversions – Minor 6th add 9th

E♭m6/9
E♭ Minor 6th add 9th
(1st inversion: 3rd as bass note)

Chord Spelling
♭3rd (G♭), 5th (B♭), 6th (C),
1st (E♭), 9th (F)

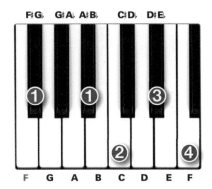

Em6/9
E Minor 6th add 9th
(1st inversion: 3rd as bass note)

Chord Spelling
♭3rd (G), 5th (B), 6th (C#),
1st (E), 9th (F#)

Fm6/9
F Minor 6th add 9th
(1st inversion: 3rd as bass note)

Chord Spelling
♭3rd (A♭), 5th (C), 6th (D),
1st (F), 9th (G)

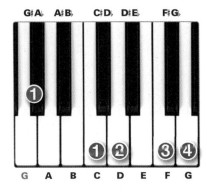

First Inversions – Minor 6th add 9th

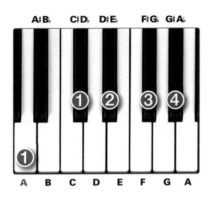

F#m6/9
F# Minor 6th add 9th
(1st inversion: 3rd as bass note)

Chord Spelling
b3rd (A), 5th (C#), 6th (D#)
1st (F#), 9th (G#)

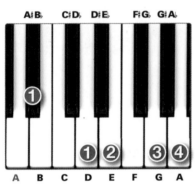

Gm6/9
G Minor 6th add 9th
(1st inversion: 3rd as bass note)

Chord Spelling
b3rd (Bb), 5th (D), 6th (E),
1st (G), 9th (A)

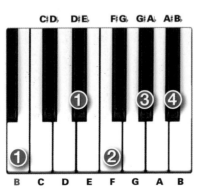

Abm6/9
Ab Minor 6th add 9th
(1st inversion: 3rd as bass note)

Chord Spelling
b3rd (Cb), 5th (Eb), 6th (F),
1st (Ab), 9th (Bb)

First Inversions – Minor 6th add 9th

Am6/9
A Minor 6th add 9th
(1st inversion: 3rd as bass note)

Chord Spelling
♭3rd (C), 5th (E), 6th (F♯),
1st (A), 9th (B)

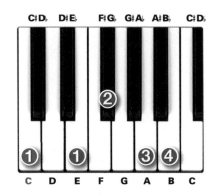

B♭m6/9
B♭ Minor 6th add 9th
(1st inversion: 3rd as bass note)

Chord Spelling
♭3rd (D♭), 5th (F), 6th (G),
1st (B♭), 9th (C)

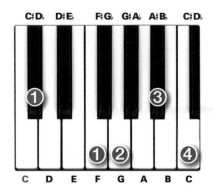

Bm6/9
B Minor 6th add 9th
(1st inversion: 3rd as bass note)

Chord Spelling
♭3rd (D), 5th (F♯), 6th (G♯),
1ot (B), 9th (C♯)

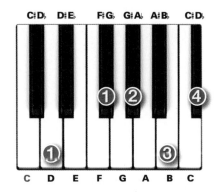

First Inversions – Major 9th

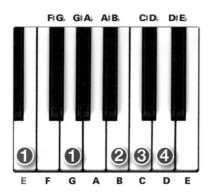

Cmaj9
C Major 9th
(1st inversion: 3rd as bass note)

Chord Spelling
3rd (E), 5th (G), 6th (B),
1st (C), 9th (D)

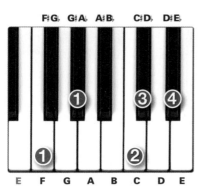

C♯maj9
C♯ Major 9th
(1st inversion: 3rd as bass note)

Chord Spelling
3rd (E♯), 5th (G♯), 6th (B♯)
1st (C♯), 9th (D♯)

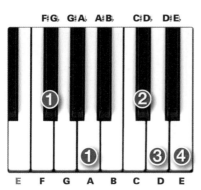

Dmaj9
D Major 9th
(1st inversion: 3rd as bass note)

Chord Spelling
3rd (F♯), 5th (A), 6th (C♯),
1st (D), 9th (E)

First Inversions – Major 9th

E♭maj9
E♭ Major 9th
(1st inversion: 3rd as bass note)

Chord Spelling
3rd (G), 5th (B♭), 6th (D),
1st (E♭), 9th (F)

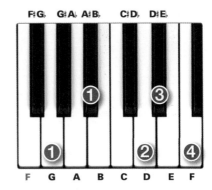

Emaj9
E Major 9th
(1st inversion: 3rd as bass note)

Chord Spelling
3rd (G♯), 5th (B), 6th (D♯),
1st (E), 9th (F♯)

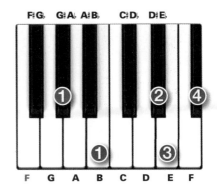

Fmaj9
F Major 9th
(1st inversion: 3rd as bass note)

Chord Spelling
3rd (A), 5th (C), 6th (E),
1st (F), 9th (G)

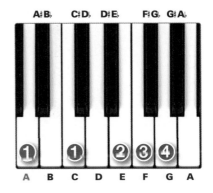

First Inversions – Major 9th

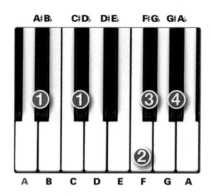

F♯maj9
F♯ Major 9th
(1st inversion: 3rd as bass note)

Chord Spelling
3rd (A♯), 5th (C♯), 6th (E♯),
1st (F♯), 9th (G♯)

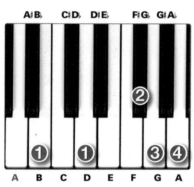

Gmaj9
G Major 9th
(1st inversion: 3rd as bass note)

Chord Spelling
3rd (B), 5th (D), 6th (F♯),
1st (G), 9th (A)

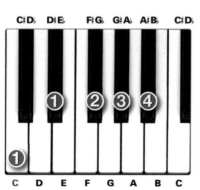

A♭maj9
A♭ Major 9th
(1st inversion: 3rd as bass note)

Chord Spelling
3rd (C), 5th (E♭), 6th (G♭),
1st (A♭), 9th (B♭)

First Inversions – Major 9th

Amaj9
A Major 9th
(1st inversion: 3rd as bass note)

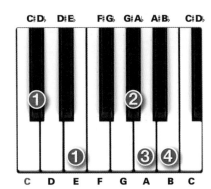

Chord Spelling
3rd (C#), 5th (E), 6th (G#),
1st (A), 9th (B)

B♭maj9
B♭ Major 9th
(1st inversion: 3rd as bass note)

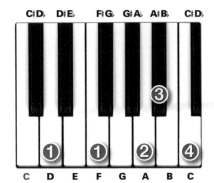

Chord Spelling
3rd (D), 5th (F), 6th (A),
1st (B♭), 9th (C)

Bmaj9
B Major 9th
(1st inversion: 3rd as bass note)

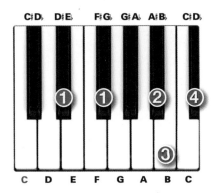

Chord Spelling
3rd (D#), 5th (F#), 6th (A#),
1st (D), 9th (C#)

First Inversions – Minor 9th

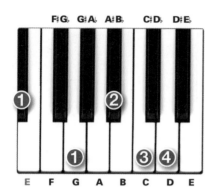

Cm9
C Minor 9th
(1st inversion: 3rd as bass note)

Chord Spelling
♭3rd (E♭), 5th (G), ♭7th (B♭),
1st (C), 9th (D)

C#m9
C# Minor 9th
(1st inversion: 3rd as bass note)

Chord Spelling
♭3rd (E), 5th (G#), ♭7th (B),
1st (C#), 9th (D#)

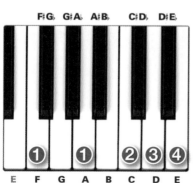

Dm9
D Minor 9th
(1st inversion: 3rd as bass note)

Chord Spelling
♭3rd (F), 5th (A), ♭7th (C),
1st (D), 9th (E)

First Inversions – Minor 9th

E♭m9
E♭ Minor 9th
(1st inversion: 3rd as bass note)

Chord Spelling
♭3rd (G♭), 5th (B♭), ♭7th (D♭), 1st (E♭), 9th (F)

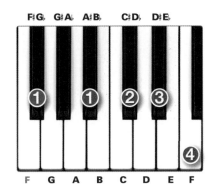

Em9
E Minor 9th
(1st inversion: 3rd as bass note)

Chord Spelling
♭3rd (G), 5th (B), ♭7th (D), 1st (E), 9th (F♯)

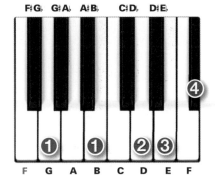

Fm9
F Minor 9th
(1st inversion: 3rd as bass note)

Chord Spelling
♭3rd (A♭), 5th (C), ♭7th (E♭), 1st (F), 9th (G)

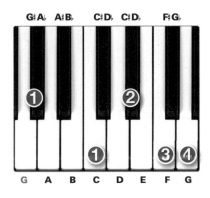

First Inversions – Minor 9th

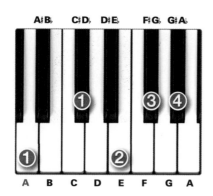

F#m9

F# Minor 9th
(1st inversion: 3rd as bass no

Chord Spelling
♭3rd (A), 5th (C#), ♭7th (E)
1st (F#), 9th (G#)

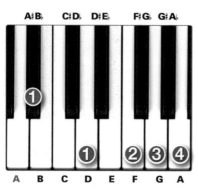

Gm9

G Minor 9th
(1st inversion: 3rd as bass no

Chord Spelling
♭3rd (B♭), 5th (D), ♭7th (F)
1st (G), 9th (A)

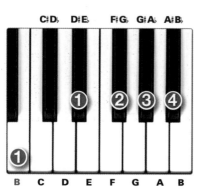

A♭m9

A♭ Minor 9th
(1st inversion: 3rd as bass no

Chord Spelling
♭3rd (C♭), 5th (E♭), ♭7th (G♭)
1st (A♭), 9th (B♭)

First Inversions – Minor 9th

Am9
A Minor 9th
(1st inversion: 3rd as bass note)

Chord Spelling
♭3rd (C), 5th (E), ♭7th (G),
1st (A), 9th (B)

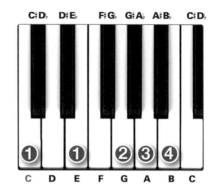

B♭m9
B♭ Minor 9th
(1st inversion: 3rd as bass note)

Chord Spelling
♭3rd (D♭), 5th (F), ♭7th (A♭),
1st (B♭), 9th (C)

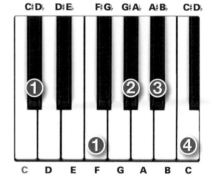

Bm9
B Minor 9th
(1st inversion: 3rd as bass note)

Chord Spelling
♭3rd (D), 5th (F♯), ♭7th (A),
1st (D), 9th (C♯)

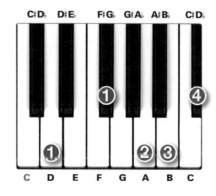

Further Reading and other useful internet resources for this book are available on **www.flametreemusic.com**

Advanced Piano Chords is another in our bestselling series of easy-to-use music books designed for players of all abilities and ages. Created for musicians by musicians, these books offer a quick and practical resource for those playing on their own or with a band. They work equally well for the rock and indie musician as they do for the jazz, folk, country, blues or classical enthusiast.

FlameTreeMusic.com

Flame Tree Music offers useful, practical information on chords, scales, riffs, rhymes and instruments through a growing combination of traditional print books and ebooks.

Books in the series:

Advanced Guitar Chords; Beginner's Guide to Reading Music; Guitar Chords; Piano & Keyboard Chords; Chords for Kids; Play Flamenco; How to Play Guitar; How to Play Bass Guitar; How to Play Piano; How to Play Classic Riffs; Songwriter's Rhyming Dictionary; How to Become a Star; How to Read Music; How to Write Great Songs; How to Play Rock Rhythm, Riffs & Lead; How to Play Hard, Metal & Nu Rock; How to Make Music on the Web; My First Recorder Music; Piano Sheet Music; Brass & Wind Sheet Music; Scales and Modes.

For further information on these titles please visit our trading website: www.flametreepublishing.com